教室の音声学読本

英語のイントネーションの理解に向けて

伊達 民和 著

英文校閲 朗読 **Bill Rockenbach**　　朗読 **Warren Wilson**

大阪教育図書

目　次

推薦のことば ... 1

序　論 ... 2

第 1 章：英語のイントネーションの概論 ... 11

第 2 章 ... 25

- 課題 1　Where is John Smith? のイントネーション ... 28
- 課題 2　Who IS he? vs. Who is HE? ... 31
- 課題 3　Where is EVerybody? vs. Where IS everybody? ... 34
- 課題 4　イギリス英語の yes-no question ... 36
- 課題 5　注意しなければいけない否定文 ... 39
- 課題 6　Adverbs of manner or degree ... 42
- 課題 7　Adverbs of time ... 44
- 課題 8　Adverbs of place ... 48
- 課題 9　You are what you eat. ... 50
- 課題 10　It is quite good. の意味 ... 52
- 課題 11　会話伝達文のイントネーション ... 54
- 課題 12　Excuse ME. と Excuse YOU. ... 56
- 課題 13　You are a dark horse! ... 59
- 課題 14　相手の反応を窺うイントネーション ... 62
- 課題 15　I don't want a ticket. ... 65
- 課題 16　I left it somewhere. ... 67
- 課題 17　新情報 vs. 既知情報 ... 69
- 課題 18　慣用的表現 I know. と I don't know. ... 73
- 課題 19　句動詞の強勢 ... 76
- 課題 20　Adverbs of place（再訪） ... 79
- 課題 21　The house is on the hill. vs. The house is on fire. ... 81
- 課題 22　That's funny. ... 83
- 課題 23　下降＋上昇調の返答文 ... 86
- 課題 24　前置詞に置かれる不可解な文強勢 ... 88

課題 25	文頭における高いピッチ：その問題点	92
課題 26	賛同、激励、賞賛を表す決まり文句	95
課題 27	Obvious questions	98
課題 28	double words の強勢	100
課題 29	What is that? の 3 種のイントネーション	102
課題 30	既知情報を伝える低上昇調	105
課題 31	冠詞の強勢	108
課題 32	What is Mary doing?	111
課題 33	Yes-no question のイントネーション	114
課題 34	Thank you. のイントネーションの諸相	116
課題 35	不定代名詞の強勢	119
課題 36	『千の風になって』	122
課題 37	than の弱形 vs. 強形	125
課題 38	音調単位の区切り	128
課題 39	代名詞の対比用法	131
課題 40	EP における対比強勢の諸相	133
課題 41	暫定的な気持ちを伝えるイントネーション	136
課題 42	句動詞の commands	139
課題 43	What language do you speak to each other?	141
課題 44	end focus「文末焦点」	144
課題 45	event sentence「出来事文」	147
課題 46	文末の副詞（再訪）	150
課題 47	polite correction のイントネーション	153
課題 48	I know her. の特異なイントネーション	156
課題 49	I thought it was going to rain.	158
課題 50	be 動詞の強勢	160
課題 51	助動詞と代名詞の強勢（再訪）	163
課題 52	Thank you VERy (SO) much.	168
課題 53	イントネーションが意味を区別する	170
課題 54	No, it isn't. vs. No, it is not.	172
課題 55	再帰代名詞の文強勢の有無	174

課題 56	単語中に起こる強勢移動	176
課題 57	名目上の subject + predicate のイントネーション	179
課題 58	Here you are. のイントネーション	182
課題 59	The books are here. vs. We have some books here.	184
課題 60	呼びかけ、警告、または、叱責のイントネーション	186

第 3 章 ……………………………………………………………… 189
 part 1: 朗読課題 ……………………………………………… 192
 part 2: 解　説 ………………………………………………… 197

まとめ ……………………………………………………………… 205

あとがき …………………………………………………………… 209

経　歴 ……………………………………………………………… 210

序　文

推薦のことば

John Wells
ロンドン大学名誉教授

　Is English intonation an important part of its phonetics? Yes, it is! Is it a pity that teachers and learners neglect it? Yes, it is! Is intonation something obscure and difficult? No, it isn't! In this book Date *sensei* explains why, and offers clear explanations of what is involved.

　The best plan for learners is to concentrate on what can readily be understood and learnt. So you should concentrate on tonicity (also known as accentuation or placement of the nucleus or tonic), which means picking out the important words in the utterance. This is more sensible than worrying too much about the choice of tone (fall, rise, or fall-rise), since many English sentences can be acceptably spoken with any tone.

　Which words need to be accented? This book tells you.

推薦のことば

三浦　弘
日本実践英語音声学会会長
専修大学教授

　円滑なコミュニケーションにはイントネーションの知識が必要ですが、イントネーションが教育現場で教えられることは少ないと思われます。そのため会話で違和感を覚えても、自分が間違った強勢配置をして話したためだとは気づきにくいものです。本書は英語イントネーションの学習に役立つ簡便でパイオニア的な教材です。「概論」を読んでイントネーションの枠組みを理解したら、「課題」を吟味して学習し、CD 音声をリピーティングすれば、イントネーションの習得も容易になることでしょう。

　著者伊達民和先生には 2018 年 10 月 27 日創立の日本実践英語音声学会（PEPSJ「ペプスィ」）の顧問として実践的な英語音声の普及にご尽力いただい

ております。以下に同学会の設立趣旨を引用させていただきますが、読者の皆様が本書を通じて英語運用能力を一層高められることを願ってやみません。

「2020年度からの小学校「外国語科」の開始や大学入試におけるスピーキングを含めた4技能評価による英語外部試験導入に伴い、今後の日本の英語教育において音声教育は非常に重要になると考えられます。このような状況に鑑み、小学校から大学までの英語教育に携わる指導者、研究者が一同に会し、英語音声教育について情報を交換し、討議し、学び合う場として新学会「日本実践英語音声学会」を設立することにしました。日本実践英語音声学会は、英語音声学・音韻論の理論と応用研究に加えて、実践的な英語発音教育を重視した活動を行います」。（http://pepsj.org/）

序　論

　私が知る限りでは、英語のイントネーションに特化した和書が世に最後に出てから久しい。渡辺和幸『英語のイントネーション論』（研究社 1994）以来、新しい著書が出ていなかった。英語のイントネーションは、研究分野が広く、かつ、奥深くて、ノン・ネーティブスピーカーの研究者が立ち入るには度胸がいる。大海原を小舟で進むような感じがする。また、日本人は、ネーティブスピーカーに生来に備わった言語的直感というか洞察力がないので、どうしても彼らの後塵を拝する感じがする。このようなことを考えると、『英語のイントネーション論』は非常に意義深い研究書であり、緻密なデータの physical evidence を収集し、それに著者独自の洞察が織り込まれている。また、姉妹編『英語のリズム・イントネーションの指導』も福音である。とは言え、中高の英語教員が手元に置いておき、日頃、困ったときに利用するという本でもない。視点を変えてみると、日頃から教科書に準拠した音声資料で聞く「不可解な」イントネーションに当惑している英語教師にとっては、first aid になる本ではない。率直に言って、指導書は全くの役立たずである。

　海外に目をやり、英語圏の EFL, ESL 講師は、どのように発音指導に取り組んでいるのだろうか、彼らの指導法から何を学べるのだろうかと期待を寄せると、意外かもしれないが、寒々とした現状である。私は、a closed international e-mail list（SUPRAS）に属している（"people concerned with problems of teaching English pronunciation ... Most of the members are authors of books or articles on the subject, but all have devoted much serious professional thought to it."）。会員になってからもう20年近くなる。このグループでは、5，6年ごとにESLとEFLにおける発音指導の嘆かわしい実態について活発な意見交換が起こる。少しづつ新しい会員が加わっているから、同じテーマが蒸し返しになるのだろう。私は、かつてはdiscussionには参加していたが、今では「またか！」という気持ちで、もっぱらいろいろな意見を読んでいるだけである。どんな内容であるか、その一部を紹介しよう。

1. A teacher has asked me why pronunciation is not taught or not prioritized in ESL teacher training courses. She has recently completed a Masters of TESOL and was quite frustrated that the course included virtually no content on teaching and learning pronunciation. Do you have any thoughts on this?

2. I have found that teachers in New Zealand often lack both the knowledge of phonetics and phonology as well as the knowledge (or confidence) of how to teach pronunciation, and those who did learn about phonetics and phonology are also often not confident that they know how to teach it. Part of the problem is that they have not all done a Masters in Applied Linguistics and so are relying on what they learned in an intensive four-week introductory course, or on a Diploma. This is perhaps not surprising (that teachers are not well qualified), given that many of these teachers are not well paid.

3. Pronunciation is under-represented in a lot of teacher training courses. In a study we did a few years ago we investigated how many Canadian universities offered pronunciation-specific courses and only six did. I agree that it is also important that teachers receive pronunciation courses that include phonetics and phonology (or have such courses as prerequisites) but that also include practical pedagogical advice...preferably with some sort of chance to apply such knowledge during the course.

4. When I go to conferences in the USA I always hear people complain that programs do not include separate grammar and pronunciation classes. I think there are different reasons for this. Many Master's programs in the USA (and

other places) are pressured to shorten their programs. The market now pushes for one-year programs. Pronunciation (and often grammar) do not fit into the required courses. Our university wants 11 courses (33 credit hours) for Master's degrees. I cannot require my pronunciation class for the degree.

5. In the US, beyond being a native speaker/pronouncer, most teachers never had to consciously learn/study pronunciation so they have no framework experience from which to gauge how to teach it. Plus, there's also the erroneous belief that if you are a native speaker, that's all you need to be an effective teacher.

6. We found only 6 universities in all of Canada that offer courses in teaching L2 pronunciation. And to offer such a course you need an instructor with the background to teach it. Even where it is taught, it is often an option rather than a required course, which suggests it isn't viewed as essential.

7. Here is another related issue: language teachers and university professors (apart from those of us who have chosen this area) tend not to spend much time on pronunciation.

　今日、発音指導はデリケートな問題である。ESL や EFL の授業では、ネーティブ・スピーカー講師は、意思疎通（intelligibility）が可能でありさえすれば、生徒・学生の発音を矯正することを遠慮している。それは、"politically incorrect" であると考えられ、差別的や人権侵害になるかもしれないからである。しかし、その一方では、社会的成功のために標準英語発音を習得したい人たちも多くいる。これは皮肉なことである。発音の「矯正（correction）」に代わって accent reduction とか accent adjustment といった婉曲表現が使われている。

　このような実情なので、アメリカやオーストラリアに語学留学しても、ESL や EFL クラスでは、まともな発音指導がなされていない。実際、私は、現役のとき、アメリカ、オーストラリア、イギリスの大学での語学研修（3 週間）に何回も学生を引率したが、まとまった発音指導の授業はなかった印象をもっている。その理由は、上記の報告から容易に推測できる。ネーティブ・スピーカー講師は、個々の単語の発音はともかく、イントネーションの体系的な指導は「不可能」と思っているようである。それは、教室外で聞いて慣れるも

のだと言う。かつて面白い表現を目にした。"Intonation is a Cinderella or a step child in ESL." John Wells が何と言っているか、もう一度序文を読んで欲しい。

　数年前の9月に名古屋で発音ワークショップの講師を務めた。それは、「GDM英語教授法研究会」が30年以上にも亘って東京で実施している定例の研修会に参加した名古屋在住の2名の人が、自分たちの勉強会の仲間に呼びかけて集まった自主研修会であった。参加者8名の女性たちは、TOEIC900以上の実績と事前に聞いていたが、プロの同時通訳者を含め、皆さんは自己紹介などで流暢な英語を話されていた。このグループにとって、イントネーションを体系的に練習したのは初体験とのことであった。そのせいか、発音に関する思い込みが、短い会話テキストの朗読演習の中でいくつか露呈した。参加者の大半が文脈に構わず否定語に核強勢を置いて読んでいた。このような傾向は、過去のセンター試験で受験者の約9割に如実に見られた。実は、SUPRASへの私のpostingを見て、Wellsが、数年後の著書 *English Intonation* (p.13) で敷衍している。発音ワークショップでは他にも、これまでの思い込みによる誤解のために、我流の読み方をするケースがあった。皆さん、イントネーションの基本規則を学ぶ必要性を痛感されたようだった。

　教師の中では、English intonation is unteachable as well as unlearnable in class. という悲観論があるが、実際には、もっと希望がもてる学習目標である。イントネーションにおける核強勢（nucleus, tonic）に関する比較的明解な規則を学べば、自分が上達していくのが実感できる。ところが、英語教師の大部分が、「核強勢」という用語を聞いたことがない。教育委員会の夏季英語教員研修で講義するとき、冒頭で私は、必ず「核強勢ということばを聞いたことありますか」と尋ねた。驚くことに毎回、9割近い受講者が、Noと言っていた。核強勢は、イントネーションという「山」の頂上に至る登山口である。登山口の存在を知らないから、山は unclimbable と諦めるのである。但し、核強勢に焦点を置いたイントネーションを学んで、「なるほど、そうか」と膝を打っても、内容が脳裏に "sink in" するには、半年くらいの間隔を置いて同じ内容の研修をもう2回ほど受講する必要があると、リピータの人びとが口々に言う。これは、歴年のコンセンサスがある事実である。英語のイントネーションは、理論的な積み上げ練習を通して飛躍的に上達することが可能である。

　英語の教職課程の必修科目から英語音声学が外されてしまい、教職課程履

修者のみならず英語教員までも、一丁目一番地である「核強勢」のことを知らない。英語音声学は、シンデレラのような不遇な境遇にある一方で、企業と行政の癒着が疑われるほど TOEIC が世を席巻している。なぜ文科省は、これほど TOEIC を「寵愛する」のか。上記の名古屋グループのような high achievers は、絶え間ない実地研修 field experience を通して、英語運用力を磨いている。しかし、大半の高得点者は、いわばペーパードライバーのようであり、会社では「使い物にならない」という声をよく聞く。まともな英語を話せない、書けないからだ。

　私の旧来からの友人で、外資系企業の顧問をしている国際派ビジネスマン（S 君）がいる。数年前、Osaka YMCA old boys' network を通して、40 年ぶりに再会した。宴たけなわの時、酒で勢いづいた S 君は、大学で TOEIC の授業をやっているのを「愚行」と言い、あれは反射神経を試すテストであって、早く英語教育界から追放するべきだと息巻いた。周囲にいた他の旧友たちにも「そうだ、そうだ」と同調する人がいた。彼らは、現役時代に商社マンとして実業の世界で英語を駆使していた企業戦士であった。それに対して、「虚業」の世界で生きてきた私は、まことに肩身が狭い思いであった。YMCA 同窓会では、私が最年長者で、彼らよりも少なくとも 6，7 歳上であった。実は、私は、1970 年大阪万博が開催される前後の時代に、YMCA の英語学校会話科で彼らを教えていた。当時は、高度成長期にあって、商社が就職先として最も人気のある企業であった。巷の英語学校は大盛況であった。今では、彼らは「恩師」を追い越した錚々たる英語の使い手であろう。

　私は、S 君の鋭い舌鋒に防戦もできず、全くお手上げであった。言い足りなかったのだろう、後日、メールが届いた。

　　… 日本人はわずか。大多数は現地の人達＋欧州は雑多。もちろん米国時代には米人だけでなく帰化したフィリピン人、ベトナム人等も数多くいましたから、最初から 24 時間×365 日、英語でスタート、英語で終わり。日本語は、日本人だけの飲み屋と自宅だけ。小生の今の会社は、本来、外資系企業だったため、TOEIC の高得点者がワンサカいます。800 点以上の取得者だけでも 25 人。内 990 点の満点保持者が 3 名。しかし、こんなに「英語が出来る」社員がいながら、海外出張に派遣できる社員、英語で相手と交渉可能な社員は 2 名だけ。残りの 23 名の社員は碌に喋れない、書かせても支離滅裂、単語のミススペルは当り前。更に残りの 225 名の社

員に至っては、英語などは全くダメ。海外拠点を作っても駐在で派遣できる社員がいない。誰にしようかと迷うどころか、そもそもいない。こういう実態を知っているので、楽天、ユニクロの社内英語統一論には全く反対です。会議での英語使用の非効率はその最たるものでしょう。

　これも小生の会社の実話です。会議で1人でも日本語が分からない人が混じる場合は「全て英語で行う」のが世界のグローバル企業の常識だから、会議の冒頭から3日間、全ての会議は英語でやることに決定。参加者は各拠点長（社長）＋営業部長（現地の人達）が多いので、当然、日本語はダメ。総勢20名弱。ここに日本の各本部からの参加者、事務局などを加えると会議全体は40名ほど。全体40名、日本語不可者5－6名。最初は、皆頑張っていたが、次第に疲労感。自分の思い、言いたい事を上手く表現できずにイライラ感が募り、最後は会議終了後に、別途、日本語で本社の我々に説明する始末。これが実態です。非効率の典型でしょう。だから楽天とかユニクロなどに騙されてはいけない。恰好をつけているだけ、マスコミが無責任に煽っているだけのこと。

　小生自身は一度も受験したこともないのに、これまで長い間社員に取得を呼びかけてきました。あの「黒マークで塗りつぶす」事が嫌いで。それがどんな問題か、どのような雰囲気でやるのか？ listening などはどういう環境の下でやるのか？ 興味が湧き、顧問に引いたのを良い機会に2016年12月に受験した。結果は840点。左耳が遠くて listening が低い。感想は、英検1級より単語の数、文章の難易度は遥かに低いですね。満点も取れないくせに批評だけは一人前です。これでは想像していた通り満点でも英語を使えないと確信しました。

　TOEICなどは民間の英語業者が金儲けのビジネスとしてやっているだけ。その問題集とやらも実際の試験の中身と殆ど同じ構成、同じ設問だから、何度か受検すると要領が会得できて、3時間の持ち時間内に全てを回答可能になる。次第に点は上がるだけのこと。知り合いの人がこれでマスターした。彼に1つのテーマで思っている事を2－3枚で writing をしてもらうと、文章にならず、論理的な構成にもならず、支離滅裂だった。

　何が大事と言って、この「きちんとした文章が書けるかどうか」。これが最も大事。米国でも英国でも「自分の言いたい事、考えている事を logical にきちんと文章で書ける能力があるかどうか」が全て。これは大学でも

ビジネスでも全く同じです。交渉時でもその場で minutes なり、MOU/MOA (Memorandum of Understanding /Memorandum of Agreement) のドラフトを書いてお互いに確認サインし、後で正式にタイプして交わすとか、メールでの交渉でもきちんと交信するのが普通。speaking も大事ですが、writing 能力は必須です。

　毎回毎回、"衝撃的な"事を書いて済みません。でも小生が書いている事は決して飛躍もせず、浮かれもせず、ごく普通の感覚で書いていますけどね。大学の先生が一番声を大にして TOEIC を非難すべきではないでしょうかね。非難はしなくとも大学で TOEIC など教えてはいけません。今大学では TOEIC を教えているんですか？　信じられないです。就活に必須であれば、それは学生が自分で勉強することであって、大学で教えることではないと思います。これ以上メールをかわすとプッツンしそうだから、ここら辺りで擱筆としましょうか。伊達さんとはこれまで全くこのような会話をしたことがなかったので色々新鮮でした。

　とんでもない脇道に逸れていまい、読者からは批判を受けるかもしれないが、このような赤裸々な事実を紹介することによって、学習者に英語学習の「王道」に戻って欲しいからである。英語を書くときも話すときも、「文法」の力がなければならない。「音法」も必要だ。しかし、世間には「文法が邪魔して、自由に話せない」と思い込んでいる人が五万といる。大相撲の力士を見よ、教科書がなくても、驚異的なスピードで日本語を喋れるようになるではないか。英語の教師は、一体何をしているのか。

　しかし、中学校と高等学校での総英語授業時間は、6 年間で約 600 時間、大学の授業を入れても、せいぜい 1,000 時間程度である。これは日常生活の約 42 日分でしかない。相撲の外国人力士が示す驚異的な日本語習得は 1,000 時間どころではない。生活を賭けて死に物狂いの努力の成果である。四六時中、日本語漬けである。僅か 1 月半分の英語学習では、たとえ片言でもコミュニケーションができるはずがない。だから学校は基礎を教えるところである。東京オリンピックに向けての英語教育を目標とするものでない。文法の学習段階を無視した対話文を機械的に暗記という、ライブではない会話練習はあまりにも空しい。学校では、文法英語の語順や枠組みを教え、使い方のルールを教える。ところで、コミュニケーション重視の一環として、センター試験にリスニングを導入した

けれども、日本人のリスニングの力は上がっていないという学会発表がある。高校では、受験対策としてリスニングの授業が行われているだけである。1989年告示の中学校学習指導要領から以降、文法・読解中心主義が否定され、コミュニケーション重視の英語教育をするようになったが、上滑りの学習になっているように思える。これが見直される日が早く来ることを願っている。

　本書は、今回の出版のために書き下ろしたものではない。実は、GDM 英語教授法研究会の月刊 Newsletter 誌上において 2005 年以来、今日まで連載してきた「音声」の記事を取捨選択し加筆修正したものである。連載は、2019 年 4 月現在で 171 号に達している。内容は、個々の語の発音、強勢、リズム、イントネーションに関したものだが、今回は、紙面の都合で、強勢とイントネーションに絞った。なお、本書には、多くの文献からの引用、海外の研究者との個人的な意見交換、SUPRAS（a closed international e-mail list of phoneticians）上での意見交換の内容が織りこまれているが、一部の人を除いて、名前は明かさない。Wells と私信交換の引用が非常に多いが、了承を得ている。また、GDM 英語教授法の教科書となっている *English Through Pictures* 1 & 2 からの引用も多い。その際は、大抵は絵を伴っているので、直ぐに EP（略語）だと分かる。

　今回の出版は、GDM 英語指導法研究会からの資金援助によるものである。衷心より感謝のことばを捧げたく思う。また、今日まで 15 年間のニューズレターへの原稿を整理してくださった中山滋樹さんにも御礼を申し上げる。大変な御苦労にもかかわらず、紙面の制限のため、今回は 3 分の 1 しか掲載できないことをお詫びしなければならない。

本書を、元「日本英語音声学会」会長都築正喜先生に捧げます。
都築先生は、平成7（1995）年に学会を創設され、会長を23年間努められた。その間、日本学術会議に加盟・登録し、日韓合同英語音声学セミナーの開催をはじめ、学会の発展に尽力されました。その御貢献に感謝し、益々のご健勝とご多幸を祈念します。

第1章：英語のイントネーションの概論

はじめに

どの言葉にもイントネーションがある。ただ、イントネーションが、意思疎通にどの程度の重い役割を果たすかという点になると、言語の間に相違が出てくる。英語は、日本語と比べるとイントネーションにかなり強く依存する言語である。この違いが生じる原因の1つは、日本語には対比とか強調、あるいは敬意や謙遜などを表現する手段として、便利な「小辞」や敬語の体系など、「文字で話者の気持ちを表現できる」道具立てが豊富に揃っているので、イントネーションにあまり頼らなくてもよい。一方、英語はそうした道具立てが比較的乏しいので、イントネーションに頼らざるを得ない。学習者はそのルールをしっかり身に付ける必要がある。

1. イントネーションとは、話し言葉のメロディーのことである。そもそも intone の意味は、to speak in a way that sounds like music or chanting である。短い文は、通例、1つの音調単位（tone unit）に相当する。下図は、それを示している。音調単位中の声の高低（pitch）の変化の全体像を総称してイントネーション（抑揚）と呼ぶ。音調単位の中で情報上で重要である語は、文強勢／アクセントを受ける。例えば、下記の Let's go to a party. では、let's、go、party が文強勢を受ける。また、文強勢／文アクセントの中で最後のものを<u>核強勢</u>（nucleus）と呼ぶ。

4	Extra high				
3	High			a	PAR-
			to		
			GO		
2	Mid	LET'S			ty
1	Low				TO-
					night.

   Figure 6.17 Musical staff used to illustrate intonation
   Celce-Murcia, Brinton, Goodwin, *Teaching Pronunciation* (2nd edition)

2. イントネーションの型を選択する際に話し手が行う決定のうち最も重要なことは、<u>核強勢をどこに置くかである</u>。核強勢は、通例、音調単位中の最後

の文強勢を受ける語に置かれる。以下の例では、3つの主なイントネーションの型 — (i) 下降調、(ii) 上昇調、(iii) 下降・上昇調 — が見られる。

| You   'mustn't   \worry. | You   'mustn't   /worry. | You   'mustn't   vworry. |

　これら三者は、言語的メッセージが同じだが、話者の心構え・気持ち（attitude）が異なる。下降調は「淡々とした（中立的な）」、そして、上昇調、下降上昇調は「激励的な」である。末尾の語 worry が最も強調されて核強勢を受け、そこで急激な声の高低変化（ピッチ変化）が起こる。

　概して言えば、文中に起こるピッチ変化の一つ一つが言語的に重要なのではなく、特定の1つのピッチ変化だけが重要である。それは最後の文強勢に起こるピッチ変化である。「最も強調されて」の意味は、単に「大きな声で」というのではなく、むしろ「急激な高低変化」と「長さ」のほうが重要である。上の2図では、party と worry が核強勢を受け par-, wor- を起点として急激なピッチ変化が生じていることが分かる。このように、核強勢は、話し手が聞き手の注意を最も引き付けたい部分の中核となるものである。厳密に言うと、核強勢を受ける語は、新情報を伝える部分（領域）の最後の内容語である。以下の①、②、③では、文脈はお互いに違うけれども、話者Bでは核強勢が同じ語（Jane）に来る。

　　① A: So what's new?
　　　 B: John phoned JANE.　　（文全体が新情報）
　　② A: What did John do?
　　　 B: John phoned JANE.　　（phoned Jane が新情報）
　　③ A: Who did John phone?
　　　 B: John phoned JANE.　　（Jane が新情報）

2.　音調単位の各単語は、必ずしも同じ比重の情報を伝えるものではない。その比重は、主として、文脈や状況に依存している。例えば、朗読される物語の冒頭 It was a very cold night. では、very, cold, night が文強勢（sentence stress/accent）を受け、明瞭に発音される。一方、it, was, a は文強勢を受けず弱く短くなる。しかし、もしこの文が、会話中での How was the night? への応答ならば、very と cold だけが文強勢を受ける。また、この文が、

第 1 章：英語のイントネーションの概論

How cold was the night? への応答ならば、very だけが文強勢を受ける。また、Was it a very cold night? への応答ならば、was だけが文強勢を受ける。

また、強勢を起点として始まる下降（fall）、上昇（rise）、下降・上昇（fall・rise）などの調子は、核音調（tone）と呼ばれる。核音調には、いろいろな表記法があるが、本書では、下記の方法を使うことにする。

fall	rise	fall-rise
↘	↗	↘↗

なお、下降調は、声がいきなり下降方向に転じるのではなく、多くの場合、核音節の直前に、声がそこに向けていったん上昇し、それ以降に急激な下降に転じる。1. の模式図中の party のピッチの変化を見ると、それがよく分かる。

3. 英語のイントネーションの標準的形式は、核強勢が文末の内容語（content word）に来ることである。内容語とは、名詞、動詞、形容詞、疑問詞、指示代名詞などで、通例、文強勢を受け強調して発音される。内容語に対して、機能語（function word）がある。機能語 ── 冠詞、代名詞、前置詞、助動詞、be 動詞、接続詞、関係代名詞、目的語用法の相互代名詞と不定代名詞など ── は、通例、文強勢を受けることが少なく、弱く短く発音される。

ただし「時の副詞」（now, today, tonight, tomorrow, yesterday, yet, already, recently など）や「場所の副詞」（at the door, on your face など）は、音調単位の末尾にあるとき、通例、文強勢を受けない。1. の模式図中の tonight. がその例である。なお、核強勢に後続する部分は、尾部（tail）と呼ばれ、核音調の終結部を引き継ぐだけである。

4. 音調単位とは、1 つの核音調で言われる文や句のことである。原稿がある場合や音読される場合には、より長くなり、文強勢もより多くなる傾向がある。自然な会話では音調単位はもっと短くなり、文強勢はもっと少なくなる傾向がある。通例、1 つの音調単位には 1 〜 3（or 4）の文強勢がある。文中に、それ以上の文強勢がある場合には、2 つ、またはそれ以上の音調単位に分割される。ただし、意味単位や文法単位も音調単位の分割に関与する。

‖ This little girl | is named Mary ‖
 (2 tune units)
‖ A heavy snow | generally comes

This little girl is named Mary.

early in October ‖　(2)

‖ Which do you like better, | tea | or coffee ‖　(3)

また、初出の名詞主語は独自の音調単位を構成する。以下の各文は、2つの音調単位に分かれ、Jack と leg，bus と bus（stop）が核強勢を受ける。

　Did you hear the news? Jack | broke his leg.

　[What happened?] A big bus | pulled over to the bus stop.

このような例から、「核強勢が文末の内容語に来る」という標準パターンに合致しないケースが時々あることが分かる。

【演習】文強勢と核強勢を指摘しよう。
音声あり
　　　　　　［正解 answer keys は本章の末尾のページにある］

1. Good bye. | Thank you for a lovely evening.
2. I usually get up around six o'clock.
3. What're you looking at?
4. What're you looking up?
5. After graduation, | what do you want to be?　（be = become）
6. During the game | I hurt myself.　（再帰代名詞は動詞の目的語）
7. He couldn't help himself | and burst out crying.
8. Sorry | I made such a fool of myself. | I must have been drunk.
（再帰代名詞は前置詞の目的語）
9. The artists respect each other.
10. They're in constant contact with one another.
11. Have you done the homework yet?　（yet は「時の副詞」）
12. Hello? | Is anyone home?
13. He was with someone then.　（somebody は前置詞の目的語）
14. She's busy at work, | so she can't be here today.　（be = come, be present）
15. Ken's fun to be with.　（be = keep company）
16. He's a salesman, | so he travels a lot.　（a lot は「程度の副詞句」）
17. He's not himself recently.　（recently は「時の副詞」）
18. Trump said, | "We'll make America great again."
19. I've just read something really funny.
20. You are what you eat.　（be 動詞と動詞との対比）

21. She thought to herself, | "Something's wrong with me recently."
22. What you need now is self-confidence. You should trust yourself.
23. Put it on the table, | not beside it.
24. She had a worried look on her face.
25. [What's your job?] I haven't got a job.

5. イントネーションの主な機能

ここでは、3.で述べた文強勢の有無に関する規則から逸脱する例外的ケースを検討する。ここから以降は、記号を用いて文強勢と核強勢、音調を表すことにする。文強勢は、当該語の強勢音節の直前に記号を付記し、核強勢は、当該語の強勢音節に下線を付記する。なお、核強勢のある語（音節）は、当然、文強勢があるので、本書ではわざわざその記号を付さないことが多い。

例：'This 'little ↘↗ girl | is 'named ↘ Mary.

(i) 聞き手の注意を引きつけたい箇所を伝える。
 a. 'Put it 'under the ↘ desk, | 'not ↘ on the desk.
 b. He 'commutes to and 'from 'school by ↘ bus.
 c. A: It's ↘ cold.
    B: It's ↘ not cold.
    A: It ↘ is cold. ↘ Terribly cold.
 d. To ↗ be | or ↘ not to be, | 'that is the ↘ question. または、
    To ↗ be | or ↗ not to be, | 'that is the ↘ question.
 e. ↘ So, | my 'fellow A ↘↗ mericans, | 'ask ↘ not | what your 'country can 'do for ↘ you. | 'Ask what ↘ you can do | for your ↘ country.

(ii) 意味を区別する。
 a. ① Would you 'like ↗ tea | or ↘ coffee? (*Which one?*)
    ② Would you 'like 'tea or ↗ coffee? (*Any drink?*)
 b. ① We are ex ↘ pecting him, | ↘ aren't we?
       (*I'm almost sure, but want to make sure.*)
    ② We are ex ↘ pecting him, | ↗ aren't we? (*I'm not sure, so please tell me.*)
 c. ① She 'dressed and 'fed the ↘ baby.

　　　　② She ↘↗ dressed | and fed the ↘ baby.　(*She dressed herself and fed the baby.*)
　d.　① A: I traveled to Wales recently.
　　　　　B: ↘ Where?　(*Where in Wales?*)
　　　　　A: Bangor.
　　　　② A: I traveled to Wales recently.
　　　　　B: ↗ Where?　(*asking for a repetition*)
　　　　　A: To Wales.
　e.　① He ↘ asked himself.　(*He put the question to himself.*)
　　　　② He ˈasked him ↘ self.　(*He did the asking himself.*)
　f.　① ˈWhat's your ↘ name?　(*matter-of-fact*)
　　　　② ˈWhat's your ↗ name?　(*more polite/friendly*)
　　　　③ ↗ What's your name?　(= *I didn't catch it.*)

(iii) 言外の意味をほのめかす（imply）。
　a.　ˈThat ˈmay be ↘↗ true.　(*But it may not be true.*)
　b.　I'll ˈdo it if I ↘↗ can.　(*But it may be impossible.*)
　c.　The ↘↗ boys are here.　(*But I don't know where the girls are.*)
　d.　I ex ↘↗ pect he'll come.　(*But I can't say for certain.*)
　e.　I ↘↗ think so.　(*But I'm not quite sure.*)
　f.　I'm ˈawfully ↘↗ sorry.　(*But it couldn't be avoided.*)
　g.　I ˈcan't ˈdo it to ↘↗ day.　(*But I may be able to tomorrow.*)

(iv) 自分の感情・態度を加味する。
　a.　ˈGood ↗ bye. ˈTake ↗ care.　(*friendly or reassuring*)
　b.　You ˈmustn't ↗ worry.　(*ditto* 同上)
　c.　There's ˈno ↗ rush. ˈTake your ↘ time.　(*ditto*)
　d.　A: Sorry to be late.
　　　　B: ˈThat's ˈall ↗ right.　(*ditto*)
　e.　A: There's only instant coffee, no coffee coffee.　(i.e. *no genuine coffee*)
　　　　B: Well, ˈthat's ˈbetter than ↗ nothing.　(*ditto*)
　f.　A: I'm sorry to be so late. ˈDo for ↗ give me.　(*pleading* 懇願)
　　　　B: ˈBetter ˈlate than ↘↗ never.　(*reassuring*)

第1章：英語のイントネーションの概論

  g. Oh, ˈplease ˈstay a ˈlittle ↗longer. (*pleading*)

  h. [There's such a draught.] ˈShut the ↗door. (*request*)

6. 語用論的理由により、文強勢が抑制される

音調単位では、通例、新（初出）情報は文強勢を受け、旧・既知情報は文強勢を受けない。これを別の観点 ── 語用論 ── から見てみよう。語用論とは、言語表現とそれを用いる使用者や文脈との関係を研究する分野である。

  a. A: Shall we go there on foot?
    B: Yes, let's. I ↘love walking.

  b. A: Would you like some bacon?
    B: No, thanks. I ↘don't like pork.

  c. A: What's your job?
    B: I ˈhaven't ↘got a job. I'm be ↘tween jobs.

  d. A: Can I offer you a piece of cake?
    B: Sorry, | I ˈdon't ↘like sweets.

  e. A: What's new?
    B: We're ˈhaving a ↘barbecue at our place.

  f. A: What's going on this Friday night?
    B: There's a ↘party at my place.

  g. A: I donated the prize money to the child support center.
    B: ˈGood for ↘you. I'm proud of you.

  h. A: What's it like being a nurse?
    B: Nursing is a good job for me. I ˈlike ↘helping people.

  i. A: I'm going to a picnic.
    B: Oh, really? ˈWho's going to ↘be there? Is ↗Jane going to be there?
    A: ↘No, | she ↘isn't going to be there. She says she's busy this weekend.

【演習】文強勢と核強勢を指摘しよう。
   ［正解 answer keys は本章の末尾のページにある］

Maya: Here comes our train. Good, it's not too crowded.

Jeff: ①<u>But it seems very crowded to me.</u>

Maya: Oh, this is nothing.

Jeff: ②Do the trains get any worse than this?

Maya: Oh, yes. During the morning rush hour, ③they're twice as bad.

Jeff: Really? ④I can't imagine a train being more crowded than this.
⑤Where I'm from, we can always get a seat.

Maya: How do you get to school back home? Do you take a train?

Jeff: No, ⑥I walk to school. I live in the dormitory nearby.

7. 名詞優先主義

初出の名詞は、文中のどこにあっても、他の内容語に優先して核強勢を受ける。それ以降の述部は尾部(tail)となり核音調の終結部を引き継ぐだけである。即ち、尾部にある内容語は文強勢をもたず、pitch change を伴わない語強勢をもつだけである。以下は、種々の文構造における名詞優先の例である。

注：核音調から以降の尾部に語強勢をもつ内容語がある場合、low pitch で発音される。

(i) 叙述文（ただし、out-of-the-blue statement の場合）

a. ↘Autumn came. The ↘leaves started to fall.
b. The ↘snow | generally comes ˈearly in Oc↘tober. (2 tone units)
c. Ow! My ↘back's killing me! | My ↘feet're killing me!
d. The room's drafty. You've ˈleft the ↘door ajar.
e. Excuse me, but you've ˈspelled my ↘name wrong.
f. OK. I'll ˈkeep my ↘eyes open.
g. I need luck with this exam. ˈPlease ˈkeep your ↘fingers crossed for me.
h. She was on the ↘↗beach, | ˈwatching the ↘sun go down.
i. [What're you doing here?] I'm ˈwaiting for the ↘store to open.
j. I ˈneed to ˈhave my ↘hair cut | and my ↘face shaved.
k. I can't go skiing this next weekend; my ↘boots want mending.
l. It's freezing cold in here; the ↘windows must have been left open.

(ii) Wh- 疑問文と感嘆文

a. ˈWhat ↘language do you speak?   What language do you speak?
b. ˈWhat's the ↘weather like in your area?
c. ˈWhat an ˈawful ↘month we're having!

第 1 章：英語のイントネーションの概論

    d. ˈWhat a ˈnice ↘couple they make!
    e. So ˈhow did the ↘test go?
    f. ˈPlease be ˈcareful ⁽¹⁾what ↘company you keep.
    g. ˈWhat a ˈlovely ↘hat she is wearing!

(iii) 関係詞節
    a. Wow! ˈLook at the ˈcool ↘car he's driving! It's a Porsche!
    b. Johnny | ˈwhere's the ↘dictionary I lent you a while ago?
    c. Hello, Violet. You look good. ˈThat's ˈsome ↘dress you have on!

🔊 8.　出来事文（event sentence）
    上記の 7 で述べた名詞優先の核強勢と直接に関連するが、特に第 1 文型（S+V）によって、「状態の変化」（change of state）、特に、出現、不慮の出来事、不運、失踪の内容を伝える。やはり初出の名詞主語が核強勢を受ける。つまり、名詞主語が主情報、動詞は副次情報となる。

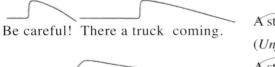

Be careful! There a truck coming.

There's a stranger at the door.

A storm is coming, I'm afraid.
(*Unfortunately, a storm is coming.*)
A storm is coming: I'm afraid.

My watch has stopped.
The train's coming.
The sun's come out.
The kettle's boiling.

    a. Sorry to be late. My ↘car broke down.
          Cf. My ↘car | got a ˈflat ↘tire.　(S+V+O)
    b. Ow, my ↘back hurts!
          Cf. Ow, my ↘back's | ˈgiving me ↘trouble again!　(S+V+O)
    c. Oh, no! The ↘store's burning!
    d. Brrr...there's a ↘cold front approaching.
    e. Look! ˈThis ↘door is falling off. It's so loose!
    f. Hang on! An ↘ambulance's on the way.　(*coming*)

g. Look! The ↘house is on fire!

    Cf. The ˈhouse is on the ↘hill.　(*no change of state; constant state*)

h. Hey, there's a mos↘quito on your arm! / There's a　↘bruise on your head.

しかし、出来事文の後に句が来る場合には、2つの音調単位になる。

```
Then a waiter comes along │ with a coffee.
```

i. Then a ↘waiter comes along │ with a ↘coffee.（上図）

j. A: What's the news?

   B: My ↘parents are here │ from ˈNew ↘York.

k. ［物語の冒頭］It was very cold, and it rained a lot that night.

   ↘Susan came home, │ ˈtired and ↘hungry.

また、第2文型（S+V+C）の出来事文もある。やはり異常事態、不慮の事故など突発的なことを伝える。

a. A: Hey, │ your ↘eyes are red!

   B: Yeah, I'm suffering from a pollen allergy.

    cf. Your ˈeyes are ↘brown │ and your ˈhair is ↘black.

      （恒常的状態 no change of state）

b. Jimmy, │ your ↘bed's messy.

c. I must get home early. My ↘daughter's sick.

    cf. My ↘daughter's │ ˈdown with the ↘flu.

d. Oh, no! My ↘wallet's missing!

e. Uh-oh. The ↘battery's dead.

f. Oh, shoot! The ↘coffee machine's out of order.　(= *not working*)

g. Oh dear, the ↘printer's jammed. I can't make copies of this.

🔊 9. 複合音調

英語には、複合音調と呼ばれる2つの核音調を含む文がある。それは、【下降調＋（低）上昇調】から成る。下降調は新情報の末尾に起こり、上昇調は旧・既知情報に起こる。後者の場合、話者が、そこに<u>多少の重要度（some degree of importance）</u>を付加している。複合音調の文は核が2つあるので、2つの

音調単位から成ると考えることができる。

a. A: Here's some chocolate, Susan.

B: Great! I ↘like | ↗chocolate.

  Cf. I ↘like chocolate. (*possible: matter-of-fact*)

b. A: Shall we go there on foot?

B: Yes, let's. I ↘like | ↗walking.

  Cf. I ↘like walking. (*possible: matter-of-fact*)

c. A: Do you like our city?

B: Yes. I ↘like it | ↗here.

  Cf. I ↘like it here. (*possible: matter-of-fact*)

d. A: I'm from Tokyo.

B: Are you? My ↘parents | were born in ↗Tokyo.

e. A: That's Jane standing at the bus stop over there.

B: Oh, I ↘know | ↗her. She's in my biology class.

f. A: Uh-oh. It's starting to rain!

B: I ↘thought | it would ↗rain.

g. A: Hello, David. Did you have a hard day at work?

B: Yeah, a bit. Ooh! The ↘soup | smells ↗good!

h. A: What sort of wine shall we have?

B: A ↘Riesling | would be ↗nice.

i. A: I've got a free day tomorrow. I want to go somewhere I've never been.

B: ↘Cambridge | is the place to ↗go.

j. A: It's started raining.

B: Mmm… They ↘promised | ↗rain.

A: Well, | they were ↘right | ↘this time.

B: I ↘hoped | they would ↗be.

==

1. 演習の **answer keys**:

 1. ˈGood ↘bye. | ˈThank you for a ˈlovely ↘evening.

 2. I ˈusually ˈget ⁽ˡ⁾up at ˈsix o' ↘clock. ⇒ **the rule of three** の適用：3つの強勢音節が隣接するとき、中間の強勢が弱化する。

21

3. ˈWhat're you ↘lookｉng at?
4. ˈWhat're you ˈlooking ↘up?
5. ˈAfter gradu↗ation,│ˈwhat do you ˈwant to ↘be?
6. ˈDuring the ↗game│I ↘hurt myself.
7. He ˈcouldn't ↘help himself│and ˈburst ⁽¹⁾out ↘crying.　⇒ the rule of three の適用
8. ↘Sorry│I ˈmade such a ↘fool of myself.│I ˈmust have been ↘drunk.
9. The ˈartists res↘pect each other.
10. They're in ˈconstant ↘contact with one another.
11. ˈHave you ⁽¹⁾done the ↗homework yet?（課題33 参照）
12. Hel↘↗lo?│Is ˈanyone ↗home?
13. He was ↘with someone then.
14. She's ˈbusy at ↘work,│so she ˈcan't ↘be here today.
15. ˈKen's ˈfun to ↘be with.　OR: ˈKen's ↘fun to be with.
　　　　　　　　　　　　　　　　（朗読の順序は逆になっている）
16. He's a ↘salesman,│so he ↘travels a lot.
17. He's ˈnot ↘himself recently.
18. ˈTrump →said,│"We'll ˈmake Aˈmerica ↘great again."
19. I've just ˈread something ˈreally ↘funny.
20. You ˈare what you ↘eat.
21. She →thought to herself, "ˈSomething's ↘wrong with me recently."
22. What you ˈneed ↘↗now│is ˈself- ↘confidence. You should ↘trust yourself.
23. ˈPut it ˈon the ↘table, ˈnot be ↘side it.
24. She ˈhad a ˈworried ↘look on her face.
25. [What's your job?] I ˈhaven't ↘got a job.

【補足説明】1と2では、正解が lovely と six ではないかと思っている人がいるだろう。勿論、それは妥当である。食事に招かれたとしよう。それが終わって暇乞いをする際に、招待主にお礼を言う状況では、Thank you for an excellent meal. をどのようなイントネーションで言うか、特にどの語に核強勢を置くか。ˈThank you for an ˈexcellent ↘meal. というべきか。しかし、この文脈では、meal は話し手と聞く手の間では shared information, common groundであるので、'Thank you for an ↘excellent meal.はどうか。後者のほうがmore logicalである。ところが、意外にも、実際の状況では、前者のほうがmore commonである。また、素敵なデートのあと、相手との別れ際に、Thank you for a lovely evening. でも、eveningはcommon groundで、分かり切ったが概念であるにもかかわらず'Thank you for an 'lovely ↘evening. と言う。

安井泉は、ある人が、学生Maryの指導教員に、What do you think of her? と尋ねた場面のことについて、以下のように述べている。

「強勢の位置は、常に意味的に予想が可能であるかというと、そうではない。予想どおりにいかない例も見られる。次の例を考えてみることにしよう。

(20) Mary is a good STUdent.

(20)については、意味的卓立は、studentではなく、goodである。「第1強勢（注：核強勢）は意味的卓立に置かれる」という原則に基づけば、(20)の第1強勢は、goodに置かれるはずであるが、そうなっていない。第1強勢は、通例、意味的卓立となっていないstudentに置かれる、意味的卓立を担っているgoodに第1強勢が置かれることはない」。『音声学』（開拓社、1992）

このように、論理的には共通知識と見なされる項目に、話し手が焦点を当てるような様々な事例がある。ある報告やニュースを聞いた時に、次のようにコメントすることがある。

'That's 'good ↘news.

天気に関するコメントとして、

It's a 'beautiful ↘day.

'What a 'lovely ↘day!

5. 演習のanswer keys:

Maya: 'Here⁽¹⁾comes our 'train. 'Good, | it's 'not ⁽¹⁾too 'crowded.

Jeff: But it 'seems very 'crowded to 'me. (OR: 'very crowded)

⁽¹⁾は、the rule of threeの影響を示す。即ち、3つの強勢音節が隣接するとき中間の強勢が弱化する。

Maya: 'Oh, 'this is 'nothing.

Jeff: Do the 'trains get any 'worse than this?

Maya: ˈOh, ˈyes. ˈDuring the ˈmorning ˈrush hour, | they're ˈtwice as bad.

Jeff: ˈReally? I ˈcan't iˈmagine | a ˈtrain being more ˈcrowded than ˈthis. Where ˈI'm from, | we can ˈalways get a seat.

Maya: ˈHow do you ˈget to ˈschool back home? Do you ˈtake a ˈtrain?

Jeff: ˈNo, | I ˈwalk to school. I ˈlive in the ˈdormitory nearˈby.

(OR: ˈdormitory nearby)

第2章

　学校で英語科教員に提供される指導書（teachers' guide/manual）の内容は、根本的に改善されるべきではないだろうか。今日、英語によるコミュニケーション能力の養成が強く求められているにもかかわらず、指導書は、現場のニーズを反映していない。指導マニュアルの基本的構成は、コミュニケーションの方法に視野を置いていない。執筆者陣は、現場の教員の声を聴取しているのだろうか。内容は、教員の要望に応えていない。昔も今も単語や句、文法、文化的情報などの解説が中心となっている。英語のプロソディ（prosody）に関する記述や解説が欠落している。

　筆者は、大学を退職するまで、友人の中高教員に頼んで指導書を見せてもらったり、出版社から入手していた。特に不満なのは、教科書準拠の音声を踏まえたイントネーションの解説がほとんど見当たらないことである。生徒を対象にした基本的パターンがあっても、教員が是非とも知っておくべき解説がない。その結果、筆者が高校教員（約15年、3校）と大阪府教育委員会事務局勤務（7年）であった頃は、ほとんどの同僚は指導書を頼りにしていなかった。多分、今も同じだろう。中高の教員は、授業中に教科書のモデルリーディングをするのが当たり前になっている。授業に行く前に教科書準拠の音声を聴き、練習をしていく。その際に、しばしば自信がない個所 — 強勢やイントネーションなど — に直面する。例えば、叙述文なのに末尾で声が低上昇している、対比でもないのに前置詞に強勢がある、句動詞は、副詞のほうが強調されるはずなのに、それが弱くなっているなど、数多くある。今日、英語教員は、TOEIC対策の勉強にかまけてきて、「音法」にまで関心が及ばず、いわば我流で発音指導をしているのではないだろうか。自分は、海外英語研修や留学の経験があり、英語で意思疎通はできると思っていても、いざ英語のpassageを朗読するときに棒読みになることが多い。「教室の音声学」が身についていないからである。実際、どのような点に留意して読むべきなのか、全く見当がつかない。英語会話能力と朗読力は、全く別の話である。以下の引用文によれば、日頃、英語で意思疎通に不自由を感じない人が、いざ英文を朗読するとき、completely unintelligibleである。引用文には誇張があるにしても、非常に不自然な読み方になることは事実である。イントネーションの「音法」が身についていないからである。

Any weaknesses in intonation are particularly noticeable in reading aloud. In extempore speech one instinctively uses the stress and intonation that best convey one's meaning and express one's feelings, but in reading aloud one is attempting to render someone else's thought, and it is therefore less easy to find the right expression. Over and over again the author has found that students who can make themselves reasonably well understood,... become completely unintelligible when they read passages from books.
    Kingdon, R. *English Intonation Practice* (1958: Introduction)

そういう私が身につまされた経験が2度ある。かつてロンドン大学英語音声学講座 (University College London Summer Course in English Phonetics　2週間) を受講したことがある。毎日、全体講義の後は10名ばかりのグループセッションがあった。期間の前半の tutor は、A *Concise Pronouncing Dictionary of British and American English* (1972) で高名な Jack W. Lewis 氏であった。彼のセッションでは、(i) intonation dictations と (ii) prosodic problem sentences のトレーニングがあった。私には冷や汗ものであった。(i) では、60項目の短い文や句が列挙された  ハンドアウトが配布され、Lewis 氏が項目ごとに2回づつ発音されるのを聴いて、参加者が、下降 (fall)、上昇 (rise)、下降・上昇 (fall・rise)、上昇・下降昇 (rise・fall) の記号を当該の単語の直前に書き込んでいく。しばしば、下降 (fall) と上昇・下降調 (rise・fall) との聞き分け、また、下降・上昇調と複合音調の「下降＋上昇調」の聞き分けが難しかった。各項目について、じっくりと考える時間や余裕もなく、次から次へと朗読されて、その都度、どの音調であったかを答えていく。私は、緊張と焦りのために最初はよく間違えていた。また、最後近くになっても、まだ間違えることがあった。(ii) では、いわゆる "normal" intonation から逸脱した35文のリストが配布され、1人1人が順々に朗読していく。これは、各文中のどの語に核強勢を置き、どのような音調で読むかを考える演習であった。例えば、

 1. Poor David's hurt himself again. — He always seems to be in trouble of some sort.

 2. I'll be with you in a moment or two. — Don't rush. We're not in a hurry,

are we?

3. I'm not the only one with that opinion. It's what most people think in this village.
4. When I was a child I spoke as a child, I understood as a child, I thought as a child; but when I became a man, I put away childish things.

これらも、じっくりと考える時間もなく、朗読していく。指名された人が文を正しく読めば、tutor による確認の後、次の文に進む。間違った読み方をすれば、tutor が訂正し、モデルを示す。毎回、50 分のセッションは非常に刺激的で、challenging でもあった。確かに、Kingdon が言うように、"reading aloud someone else's thought" を適切に朗読するのは、non-native speaker には難しいことを実感した。イントネーションは数多く聞いておれば自然に身に付くものではなく、音法を学び、徐々に積みあげていくべきものだと確信した。

2011 年には、日本英語音声学会がオーストラリアの The University of Queensland と共同企画した音声学講習にも参加して John Ingram 氏から指導を受けた。これら 2 つの研修で学んだことは、まさに eye-opening experiences であり、後の発奮材料となった。

UCL での音声学講座が契機となって Jack と頻繁なメール交換が始まった。これまで私信が多いが、時には、内容が、彼の PhonetiBlog で紹介されることもあった。本書の内容は、彼からの教示に負うところが多い。もう 90 歳を超える年齢になっておられ、健康な日々をお過ごしであることを切に願っている。

教室の音声学

課題 1　　Where is John Smith? のイントネーション

　最近は、How're you? よりも How're you doing? とか How're things? という表現をよく聞く。ちょっと面白いのは、オーストラリアでは、How're you going, mate? が Aussie English の代表として見られている。ただし、母音が英米語とは違い、how/hæʊ/, go/gʌʊ/, mate/mʌɪt/ となる。初心者が聞くと、それぞれ「ヘヤゥ」「ガゥ」、「マィト」のように聞こえる。昨年、西オーストラリアの Perth を訪問しているとき、現地の終日ツアーに参加した。観光バス（coach）に乗り込んだ時、ドライバー（運転と commentaries の両方をする）から Hi, how're you going? と挨拶された。Hi も「ホイ」/hɒɪ/ と聞えた。

　さて、How're you doing? と How're you going? では、核強勢は、定石通りに末尾の内容語（doing と going）に来る。しかし、How are you? では、文末に内容語がない。唯一の内容語は文頭の how だけである。それならば、how に核強勢が来るかというと、実際にはそうならない。*↘How're you?（不適）

　もし↘How're you? が可能である文脈があるとすれば、それは、↘Where're you? との対比しか考えられない。

Who is this?
He is John Smith.
His name is John Smith.
Where is John Smith?
He is at the door of his house.

　実は、疑問詞は、内容語の範疇にあり文強勢を受ける資格があるが、通例、文（音調単位）の冒頭では核強勢を受けないという特異な特徴がある。右図は、*English Through Pictures*（以後、EP）からである。John Smith が3度も出てくる。では、Where is John Smith? のイントネーションは、どうなるか。核強勢はどの語に来るか。日本語の感覚では ↘Where is John Smith? と言いたくなるが、実際には ˈWhere is ˈJohn ↘Smith? となる。音声資料でもそうなっている。

もう1つの疑問として3度目の語に核強勢を置くというのは理屈に合わない。それならば、代名詞を使って Where is he? のほうが自然ではないかと思われるが、実際にはそうは言えない。その理由は、次の「課題2」で述べる。

　私は、概論の中で「核強勢は、話し手が聞き手の注意を最も引き付けたい部分の中核となるものである」と述べた。それによれば、where がその候補になるはずである。実際には、そう言わない。これは論理的説明ができない。

　Logic seems to suggest that the WH-word is the focus of the question,

課題 1　　Where is John Smith? のイントネーション

and yet, in English at least, the WH-word does not normally bear the most prominent accent. That is, English has *Where are you GOING?* rather than *WHERE are you going?*

R. Ladd, *Intonational Phonology* (1996:170-171)

以下でも同じである。
- a.　A: I went shopping.
  　　B: ˈWhere did you ↘go?　　(↘Where did you go? は possible, but rare)
- b.　A: I hate him.
  　　B: ˈWhy do you ↘hate him?
  　　　　(↘Why do you hate him? は possible, but rare)
- c.　A: Who said it?
  　　B: I ˈdon't⁽¹⁾ ˈknow ˈwho ↘said it.

Notice that the nucleus and hence focus falls on previously mentioned items (old information). It is possible to put the nucleus on the new item, the wh word, but such a placement seems intuitively a less likely possibility.　　Alan Cruttenden, *Intonation* (1997:85)

次に、How are you? は、どのようなイントネーションになるか。一般には、ˈHow ↘are you? となる。では、なぜ機能語とされる be 動詞が核強勢を受けるのか。既に述べたように疑問詞は、通例、冒頭では核強勢を受けることはない。しかし、英語の文（音調単位）では、必ずどこかに核強勢を置かなければならない。その候補の語 — be 動詞か代名詞 — のどちらかに置かなければならない。もし代名詞に核強勢を置けば、他の人と対比されていると解釈されるので具合が悪い。一方、be 動詞は、それ自体に固定した単一の意味はなく、文脈によって、いろいろな意味になるので、そこに核強勢を置くのが妥当である。John Wells の解説を紹介しよう。

There are a few patterns involving the verb 'to be' in which the tonicity is not easily explained by the usual rules. They can be considered intonational idioms.... In a wh-question consisting of wh-word + verb 'to be' + pronoun, the tonic in neutral tonicity goes on the verb 'to be'.

注：tonicity とは核の配置のこと。また tonic は核強勢のこと。

ただし、皆さんも聞いた経験があると思うが、誰か親しい人に会ったときに、

冒頭から ˈHow're ˎyou? と言うことがある。これは、他者との対比ではなく、親しみを込めた言い方である。また、不審な人に対して ˈWho are ˎyou? と言う。非・対比的な代名詞の強勢については、「課題 51」で説明している。なお、蛇足になるが、音調単位の冒頭で、疑問詞が核強勢を受けない現象は、以下のような内容語を含まない疑問文でも見られる。

　ˈWhere are you ˎfrom?
　ˈWhere ˎto?
　ˈWhat ˎfor?

課題 2　　Who IS he? vs. Who is HE?

　ある日、中学校の教科書準拠の音声資料（CD）を点検していたとき、教師には不可解と思えるイントネーションを聞いた。*New Horizon* 3 と *New Crown* 3 とに共通して聞かれた。

a.
　Ken:　Do you know Kimura Mari?
　Kate:　Kimura Mari? Who is she?
　Ken:　She's the girl in the commercial for *Best Cake*.
　Kate:　Let's see. You mean the girl playing Sayaka in *School Life*?
　Ken:　Right. That's her.

　問題の個所は、2 行目の Who is she? である。多分、誰もが ꞌWho ↘ is she? となるのを期待するだろう。ところが、CD では、代名詞に核強勢を置いて ꞌWho is ↘ she? と言っている。なぜ she は、some other person との対比でもないのに、焦点 ── 核強勢 ── が置かれているのか。

　別の中学教科書 3 にも、以下の対話が載せられている。

b.　A: I'm a big fan of Ozaki Yutaka.
　　B: Ozaki Yutaka? ꞌWho is ↘ he?
　　A: He's a singer who was really popular among young people.
　　B: Let's see... Is that the man who sang *I Love You*?
　　A: Right. That's him.

ここでも Ozaki Yutaka が 2 度も言及されているので ꞌWho ↘ is he? と言ってもよさそうに思える。しかし、名前は単なるラベルであって、彼の実体を何ら伝えるものではない。B にとって、Ozaki Yutaka のことは新情報同然である。従って、B は、he に焦点 ── 核強勢 ── を置くのである。それ故に、以下のようなやりとりも考えられる。

c.　A: I'm a big fan of Ozaki Yutaka.
　　B: Who is Ozaki Yutaka?　（代名詞を使っていない）

確認のために海外の研究者にメールし、以下のような返信があった。

・My first 'reading' was *who's* \HE (focus on 'he'; fall as normal on a Wh-Q; maybe high fall to express strength of feeling ("Never heard of him").

・If I'm just referring to someone my interlocutor knows but I don't, I would ask *Who's HE?*

- B could have simply said WHO? ("I have never heard of him!") Although *Ozaki Yutaka* has been mentioned already and would therefore usually qualify as 'given' information, B decides to place his/her focus on HE, because *Ozaki Yutaka* is in fact NOT 'given' information to him/her.

注：given：既知の

d. A: Peggy's going out dancing with Woody Merrill.
   B: Oh? <u>Who is he?</u>
   A: He's Bill Merrill's son.
   B: Oh, yeah. Fine people, the Merrills.

この対話文でも Who IS he? は適切ではない。なぜならば、このパターンは、既に Woody Merrill について、既に何らかの情報が少しあり、更なる情報を求めるケースである。実際には、彼については白紙の状態である。確認のために、海外の研究者のコメントを紹介しよう。

(i) Who is HE?

(ii) Who IS he?

- To me, (i) signals that I don't know anything about the person being referred to, while in (ii) I may already have heard something about them but need more detail.

- To me, it's only (i) that seems natural. I can't seem to envision a scenario where (ii) would be likely, since the name "Woody Merrill" doesn't, at the moment of the B's reply, ring a bell for him, and thus "Who is[Who's] THAT?" (or, equivalently, "Who is[Who's] HE?") seems necessary to me.

ところで、旧版の中学校教科書 *New Horizon* 1 には

Ms. Green: OK, everyone. Let's talk with Bill.
Judy: What? <u>Who's BILL?</u>
Ms. Green: He's my brother.

ほとんどの人が、なぜ Who is he? と書かれていないのかと疑問に思うだろう。初出の Bill は藪から棒に発せられた全く未知の人物（"Never heard of him."）

課題2　　Who IS he? vs. Who is HE?

であるからである。または、話者は、本人に焦点を当てるので、Who is HE? という発音も可能である。しかし、このようなイントネーションは異例であり、英語学習入門期には不適切である。それ故に、代替の Who is BILL? と書かれている。この証しが EP Book One (p.58) にもある。

　　Who is this?
　　He is John Smith.
　　His name is John Smith.
　　<u>Where is John Smith</u>?
　　He is at the door of his house.

　He's John Smith. と言った後は、彼についての情報は何もない。John Smith は、事実上、新情報であるに等しい。従って、Where IS he? とは言えない。

　従って、見知らぬ女性をこっそり指差す時は、Who's SHE? と言う。

課題3　　Where is EVerybody? vs. Where IS everybody?

　数年前の日本英語音声学会の研究発表会でのことである。1つの発表が終わり、10分間の会場移動時間中に友人のアメリカ人と別の発表会場の教室に行ったら、誰も来ていない。その時、彼が発した言葉は、ˈWhere ↘is everybody? であった。2人ともプログラムにある会場が変更になっているのを忘れていた。もしイントネーションに関心のある人が彼の発言を聞いたならば、その intonational meaning は何だろうと思ったかもしれない。概して言えば、中立的・標準的パターンでは機能語 be は強勢を受けない。従って、普通では ˈWhere is ↘everybody? となる。

　実は、機能語が強調され話者の高揚した気持ちが表される場合がある。その場合、話者は強勢を置いた機能語そのものに関心があるのではなく、文全体に関心がある。

漫画では、男性が新しい隣人である妙齢の婦人に対して愛想をふりまいている。また、映画 *My Fair Lady* の中で上流階級の息子 Freddy が、貴婦人に変身した Eliza を紹介され ˈHow ↘do you do? と言っている。脚本のト書きには "instantly infatuated" とある。一目ぼれ（love at first sight）である。また *New Crown* I（旧版）の CD では、

　　Alice goes to Wonderland. "Oh, ˈwhat ↘is that?" she asks.
　　"An egg is on the wall!" (p.77)

また、面識のない人からの電話には、ˈWho is ↘this, ↗please? ということがあるが、不審者には ˈWho ↘is this? と言う。ここでも、やはり、the unexpectedness of the situation が反映されている。

　話は元へ戻る。会場に誰もいないのを見て、日本人なら、「どこへ」が最も重要な語であるので、多分、↘Where is everybody? と言うだろう。しかし、

課題 3　　Where is EVerybody? vs. Where IS everybody?

英語では、疑問詞に核強勢を置くのは、他の疑問詞との対比の場合である。たまたま、John Wells の phonetic blog（Monday, 6 February 2012）に類似のトピックがあることを発見した。彼が所属しているジョッギング同好会（jogging club）での話である。

> Despite a light fall of snow, I turned up at my jogging club yesterday morning as usual for the social jog. On a normal Sunday morning we expect 60 to 70 people for the social. But yesterday at starting time there were a mere 20 or so. Someone said,
>
> ⎮Where ↘ is everybody?
>
> Your task for today is to account for the tonicity of this sentence. Why does the intonation nucleus go on *is*? When I discussed this type of sentence with Japanese EFL students, they pointed out, quite rightly, that the most important word seemed to be ***where***. Why does it not bear the nucleus? The fact is that it doesn't. Not only in English, but apparently in all Germanic languages, the nucleus in this type of sentence goes on the verb 'to be' — even though, on the face of it, this word has very little semantic importance. It's not as if we were asking where everyone is as opposed to where they are not. Nor are we asking where they are as opposed to where they were. Perhaps there is no better explanation than to say that it is idiomatic.

Wells の blog に対して、読者からいろいろとコメントが発信された。その一つを紹介しよう。

> For me [American], "Where IS everybody?" works because of the unexpectedness of the situation. I'd say it if I walked into a friend's apartment and found just one person where I expected five. But if I had no particular expectation on this occasion, I might ask casually "Where's EVerybody?"

課題4　　イギリス英語の **yes-no question**

　皆さんには、イギリス人の友人や知人がいるかも知れない。耳聡い人ならば、yes/no question を発するとき、彼らのイントネーションに「ユニークな」特徴があることに気がついているかも知れない。では、イギリス人は、以下の疑問文をどのようなイントネーションで発音するだろうか。

　　Are you all right?
　　May I have the bill?
　　Is this a book?

アメリカ英語では、通常、文全体が漸次の上昇調イントネーションになり、核強勢を受ける音節で際立った声の高さの変動が起こる。これまでは、イギリス英語でも同じイントネーションになっていた。イギリス人音声学者 Jill House は、yes/no questions のイントネーションについて以下のように述べている。

- A simple <u>rise</u> is a safe choice for a genuine, polite question; a high rise sounds more casual; a <u>fall-rise</u> can sound rather curious...
- <u>Falling</u> tones are also common; they may sound more like a demand for information, and may be used by interviewers to establish a set of facts.

　　　　　　　　ロンドン大学（英語音声学）Summer Course（August 16. 2006）ハンドアウト

　さて、冒頭で述べた「ユニークな」特徴とは fall-rise（下降・上昇調）のことである。House は、それが rather curious の響きがあると述べているが、more polite とする解説もある。実は、最近、yes-no questions で核強勢音節が<u>下降・上昇調</u>になる傾向が広まっていて、既に文献や講演の中で指摘されている。具体的には、次のようなイントネーションになる。

　　May I ˈhave the ↘↗<u>bill</u>?
　　Are you ˈall ↘↗<u>right</u>?
　　Is ˈthis a ↘↗<u>book</u>?

Wells の *English Intonation*（2006）には、この新傾向に関する解説はないが、彼の *My daily phonetic blog* には数回にわたって短い言及が見られる。

- A fall-rise tone on a yes-no question is heard increasingly frequently. (July 17, 2006)
- Some speakers (particularly younger ones?) might alternatively use a

課題4　イギリス英語の yes-no question

highish fall-rise instead of a rise.　（August 16, 2006）
私は、在職中に学生の英語研修プログラムの引率者としてイギリスを訪問しているときに、現地学生が yes-no question を発するときに fall-rise の調子になっていることに気づいていた。Do you ↗ like it? ではなく、Do you ↘↗ like it? を聞いた時、何かしら大袈裟な印象を持ったことを覚えている。また、shopping mall などで耳をそばだてていると中年の人でもそのような話し方をするらしいという印象を抱いていた。次に下記の資料中の yes-no questions に付記されたイントネーションの表記を見て欲しい。

```
Harriet   Hello, David. I'll take your coat.        David    I went to a play last night.
David     Thanks, Harriet. Whew!                     Harriet  Oh. Did you enjoy it?
Harriet   Are you tired?                             David    I did. I saw some people I knew.
David     Mmm . . . a bit. Ooh! That soup smells good!  Harriet  Did you speak to them?
Harriet   Are you hungry?
David     I'm absolutely starving.
Harriet   Did everything go well?
David     Pretty well. Cor! Baked potatoes! . . .
```

単純な上昇調の表記になっていない。私たちの認識では、yes-no questions のイントネーションは「上昇調」であるが、ここでも下降・上昇調が見られる。上記の資料は、Ian Thompson, *Intonation Practice*（Oxford University Press, 1981）が出典である。正直言って、私がこの本を読み始めたとき、戸惑った覚えがある。

以下は、Peter Ladefoged（2001:12-14）からの解説文と図である。

　Questions that can be answered by yes or no, such as *Are you going away?* usually rise at the end…In this particular utterance, the last word was said with some <u>emphasis</u>, so that this tune can be characterized as a fall・rise. Unemphatic yes-no questions typically have just a rise at the end.

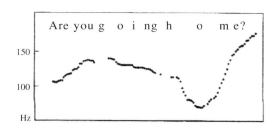

この図では、home が核強勢を受け、しかも下降・上昇になっている。Robert Ladd という著名なアメリカ人研究者がいる。彼は、長年にわたりエデ

ンバラ大学（スコットランド）で教鞭をとっている。ある時、彼は帰国した。
> When he went back to the States one time after having lived in the UK for a long time, he asked for the check in the restaurant at the end of the meal. Speaking with his American English accent, he used the polite (in British English) fall-rise on the request, "May I ˈhave the ↘↗ bill?" In return, he received a surprised, somewhat offended look from the waitress who (in his view) interpreted his question as a less than a polite request. (His interpretation of what happened was that the fall-rise was a form that would not be used in the American context on the first request, but only after the check had been requested but not brought). —Supras posting May 1, 2007

つまり、イギリス英語の下降・上昇調は、アメリカ英語では一般的ではなく、ウエートレスが驚き、気分を害してしまった。イントネーションの怖いところは、話者が意識しようと否とにかかわらず、聞き手に特定の態度を伝えてしまうことである。ウエートレスは、"May I ˈhave the ↘↗ bill?" の中に negative attitude ── 執拗さ (insistence) ──を読み取ってしまった。

　これまで、イギリス英語では、左の2図のように、高いピッチで始まり、次いで際立って下降し (step down)、最後で low rise となると言われてきた。

しかし、Geoff Lindsey, *English After RP*（2019:103-4）によると、
> This pattern can certainly be heard today, but its meaning is more marked and less neutral than it was in RP... In SSB today, a more neutral and common way of asking yes-no questions ... ends in the Fall-Rise nuclear tone rather than the Low Rise. This gives us a more straightforwardly polite yes-no question, suitable for any addressee. The Fall-Rise is very common in SSB.
> 　　　　　　　　　　　　注：SSB: Southern Standard British pronunciation

　このような新傾向の解釈について、Lindsey、Jill House、Peter Ladefoged の3者の間で見解が異なることが少し気になるが、yes-no question における Fall-Rise が広まっている。

課題 5　　　注意しなければいけない否定文

右図の場面では She does ↘not see. となることは誰でも理解できるだろう。see は situation に存在している既出語である。一方、絵にはないが、中立的な言い方である She does 'not ↘see. は、例えば、Her eyes are shut. She does not see. のような context で可能である。ところが、以下のような場面では、日本人学習者の多くが間違いを犯してしまう。

My eyes are open.
I see.
Her eyes are shut.
She does not see.

I see her.
She does not see me.

a.　A: What is your job?
　　B: *I don't have a job.*

b.　A: Have some more milk.
　　B: *I don't want any more milk.*

c.　A: Why don't you invite John to the party?
　　B: *Because I don't like John.*

d.　A: Are they her brothers?
　　B: *She has no brothers.*

彼らは、否定語を最も強調して発音してしまう。正しくは、have, want, like, has である。このようなエラーは、母語転移（F1 transfer）が影響している。日本語では、否定語が文末に来るので、特に重要であると感じられ、そのような心理が英語の否定文にも転移するのであろう。そう言えば、「日本語では、文を最後まで聞かないとイエスかノーかが分からない」と言うことがある。2002 年センター試験で約 50 万の受験者の約 86% が haven't を「最も強調して発音される語」として選んだ（河合塾大学入試研究会資料）。

　　Jim: What job do you eventually want to have?
　　Rie: I haven't thought about it.

私は、このことを John Wells に紹介すると、*English Intonation*（2006:13）で取り上げられた。

> In the corresponding Japanese sentence the last word is a negative particle such as ***nai***, which in Japanese carries the equivalent of the nucleus. So a Japanese speaker of English would tend to place the English nucleus on the word that incorporates the translation of ***nai***, namely, ***haven't***:

I haven't thought about it.
正解は、I ˈhaven't thought about it. である。英語では、否定語の後に新情報の内容語が来る場合、たとえ話者の主たる意図が否定であっても、核はその新語に来る。

　　　...if the negation word is followed by a 'new' lexical item, the nucleus goes (as normal) on that new lexical item, even though the speaker's main intent may be negation.

　　　Have some more milk.　　I ˈdon't want any more milk.　　Wells (2006:135)
　英語の母語話者は、学習者が母音および子音で苦労をすることを知っている。母語話者ではない人とのやりとりでは、母語話者は分節音の誤りは大目に見てくれるが、イントネーションの誤りは気づかない。これは、恐らく母語話者に、イントネーションにも間違いが起り得るのだという認識がないからだろう。だから、英語話者は、相手が言っている通りのことを意図していると見なしてしまう。

　アメリカの言語学者 Dwight Bolinger (1907-1991) は、英語のイントネーションの研究に多大な功績を残した。彼は、イントネーションによって表出される emotions や attitudes についても詳細な解説を行っている。その中で、あるインド人に関する興味深い記述がある。私の著書（1998）の中でも紹介している。あるインド人が、預金をするためにロンドンの銀行に行き、出納係に左図のように告げる。

```
         cuse               e                              e.
       e.              mon                  I want to deposit some       e  s
Ex   m    I want to deposit s o  e                              m o n  y. p l  a
                                          y.
```

　　　　　　　　　　　　　　　　　　　　　　　　　　　Bolinger (1989:62-63)

Bolinger によれば、銀行では money は分かり切った既知概念であるにもかかわらず、それを強調する（emphasizing the obvious）のはイギリス人には "pushiness"（強引な、厚かましい）の印象を与える。なお、ここで「強調する」というのは、new/major information を伝えるときに用いられる下降調の核強勢のことを言っている。一方、イギリス人ならば、右図のようになるだろう。末尾を低上昇調にして語調を和らげていることが分かる。もしも上記の a, b, c, d の対話においても、B が否定語を強調して言ったとすれば話者の意図はどうであれ、淡々とした中立的態度から逸脱したニュアンス ── 強い主張、

課題 5 注意しなければいけない否定文

抗議、反発など ── が伝わることになるであろう。このようなイントネーションそのものは間違いとは言えず、話者の感情・態度次第で妥当なこともある。ただ、それを知らない非母語話者が自分の意図とは違うメッセージを送ってしまうこともあり得る。

ある日本人の女子留学生に関して、次のような記述がある。

> A few years ago, while visiting relatives, I rode to a party in a car with four or five other people, one of whom was a girl of sixteen or so, an exchange student from Japan. When I got out of the car, the Japanese girl smiled at me and said, "Open the door, please."... The momentary shock of being addressed "that way" was as vivid as if she had slapped me.
>
> R. Ladd, *The Structure of Intonational Meaning* (1978:126)

一体、なぜ日本人学生の一言が、彼に衝撃を与えたのだろうか。彼によれば、Open the door, please. は、"thinly-veiled command that expects compliance"（否応なしの命令）を意味する。彼女が "Hey, could you get the door for me?" と言ってくれれば、よかったのに。さらに都合悪いことに、彼女はきっと下降調で言ったのだろう。話し言葉では、命令文に please を付加しても、丁寧な口調になるとは限らない。

> Commands ending with the word "please" are not politer than without it, if they are said with an abrupt falling nucleus:
>
> ⎜Shut the \door, please. is not polite.
>
> ⎜Shut the /door, please. is polite.
>
> M. Schubiger, *English Intonation* (1958:54)

しかし、命令文（command）であっても、相手の利益（comfort や benefit、etc.）のためならば下降調でもよい。それは無礼ではない。

a. En⎜joy your ↘ stay.
b. ⎜Take your ↘ time.
c. ⎜Help your ↘ self.
d. ⎜Come ⎜in and ⎜make yourself ↘ comfortable.

課題 6   Adverbs of manner or degree

　最近、***Eat well. Live well.*** という味の素のコマーシャルが流れている。どのようなイントネーションで言われているか。特に、どこに核強勢が来るか。言い換えると、どこで声の高さ（pitch）が目立って変化するか。2つの音調単位で言われている。‖ Eat well, | Live well. ‖ では、pitch change が動詞で起こるのか、それとも副詞で起こるのか。正解は、動詞で起こる。

　　　　　↘ Eat well. と ↘ Live well.

　しかし、ここで疑問が起こるだろう。そもそも「核強勢は、音調単位の最後の内容語に来る」という原則があるではないか。だから内容語 well が核強勢を受けるべきではないか。確かに、I'm ˈvery ↘ well. とか、He'll ˈget ↘ well. と言う。実は、well は形容詞のときは文強勢を受けるが、「程度の副詞」として他の動詞と連語になる場合は、文強勢 ── 従って、核強勢 ── を受けない。つまり、<u>動詞のほうに焦点が置かれる</u>。例えば、

　　a.　He ˈspeaks ↘ English well.
　　b.　The ˈproject ⁽¹⁾isn't ↘ going well.
　　c.　I ˈcan't ↘ sleep well lately.
　　d.　Pease speak a bit louder. I ˈcan't ↘ hear you very well.
　　e.　I ˈdon't ↘ know him very well.

なお、「順調に」（proper functioning）という意味の well に代わって properly がよく用いられるが、同義であるので、核強勢を受けない。

　　f.　He's got a backache, so he ˈcan't ↘ walk properly.
　　g.　She's hard of hearing; she ˈcan't ↘ hear properly.

しかし、ˈfeel well と ˈlook well もよく聞かれる。なぜならば、feel や look と言えば、well は予測可能であるから、文強勢を与える必要がない。
比較対照の例を挙げると、

　(i)　A: What are you using my pen for?
　　　B: Be ˈcause it ↘ writes well.

　Bolinger は、以下の解説をしている。

　It is easy to see why this type of adverb is not accented ─ it is almost redundant; in view of the context, "Because of the way it writes" gives the same information.　　*On Accents* (p. 81)

課題 6　　Adverbs of manner or degree

(ii) X: What are you using my pen for?

　　Y: Be ˈcause it ˈwrites ↘*beautifully*.

副詞 beautifully は、semantically rich であるから焦点が当たる。

そう言えば、副詞用法の a lot も「程度の副詞」である。

h. In winter I play squash. And in summer I ↘*swim* a lot.

i. He is a salesman, so he ↘*travels* a lot.

とは言え、強意用法の well と a lot は核強勢を受ける。

j. My ˈfather's ˈbusiness ˈisn't ⁽ˈ⁾going ↘*well*.

k. A: Do you get much exercise, Joe?

　　B: Yes, I do. I ˈwalk a ↘*lot*.

l. I just love to exercise. I like many different sports. Let's see… I ˈlike ⁽ˈ⁾swimming a ↘*lot*.

m. He ˈtalks a ↘*lot*, but he says nothing.

更に言うと、副詞の much についても同じである。

n. I spend a lot of time traveling, so I'm ˈnot ↘*home* very *much*.

o. I ˈdon't ⁽ˈ⁾eat ↘*out* much, because there aren't any interesting places near my apartment.

p. I like all kinds of music, but I ˈdon't ⁽ˈ⁾care for ↘*rock* very *much*.

q. A: Do you eat a big lunch?

　　B: No. I only get half an hour for lunch, so I ˈdon't ⁽ˈ⁾have ˈtime to ↘*eat much*.

　　　注：例文中で (ˈ) という記号は、直後の語の文強勢が optional という意味である。自然なスピードで発せられる文では、文強勢が3つ隣接すると英語の強弱のリズムに乗れないので、中間の文強勢を抑制する傾向がある。One, two, three や A, B, C, a big brown dog などでも、two, B, brown は弱められる。これは the rule of three「3連規則」と呼ばれる。

教室の音声学

課題 7　　Adverbs of time

　概論の中で、文末の「時の副詞」は、文強勢を受けないと述べた。日本語の感覚では、重要な意味をもつように思えるのに、なぜ文強勢を受けないのかについて説明をしてこなかった。英語話者の言語感覚では、文末の now, today, tomorrow, yesterday などは、主情報に付随する（incidental）情報であると見なされる。このことは、文頭の tomorrow と対比するとよくわかる。
"What are your plans?"
　(i)　Well, | to ↗ morrow | I'm ˈstaying ↘ home.
　(ii)　I ˈguess I'll ⁽¹⁾stay ↘ home tomorrow.
模式図で表すと、上記はそれぞれ

```
                  mórrow         stáying
Well,  to                  I'm            hó
                                              me.
```

```
                                 hóme
     guéss
I            I'll  stay               tomorrow.
```

　新情報のうちの主なものを一次情報（primary information）、付随的なものを二次情報（secondary information）と呼ぶ。二次情報は、一次情報の音調の末尾を受け継ぐ。文末に now, again と then がよく出てくるが、大抵は二次情報の扱いになっており、先行する一次情報の語に来る核音調の終結部を引き継ぐ。一方、文頭の then と now は、独立した音調単位として、上昇調、または下降・上昇調で言われる。なお、文末の again も、「元通りに」という意味の場合は、文強勢を受けないが、「もう一度」の場合は、文強勢（核強勢）を受ける。ただ、紙面上では、「どちらがどちら」であるかは判断できない。発言者の解釈に左右される。トランプ大統領の決まり文句 We'll make America great again. を聞くと、again は二次情報である。
　「時の副詞」と言うと、音声学の教本には、上記の語しか示されていないことが多いが、次に挙げる語もその範疇に入る。日本人は、already と before を「重要である」と見做し、強調して発音する傾向がある。

44

課題 7　　Adverbs of time

a. A: Rose, would you like to go out for some pizza on Saturday night?
   B: Sorry. I've ˈmade ⁽¹⁾other ↘plans *already*.
b. A: It's a pretty easy job. You just take people's dogs out for a walk twice a day.
   B: Well, I've ˈnever ↘done it *before*.
c. A: Languages are difficult to learn, aren't they?
   B: Yeah. I ˈtried to ˈlearn Japa↘nese *once*, but I gave it up.
d. A: How about your brother? ˈWhat has ↘he been doing *lately*?
   B: I don't know.
e. I run my own business and I work from my home. I ˈdon't have to ˈgo into ↘town *often*.
f. A: The show opens on Saturday morning.
   B: How about we go in the afternoon? I ˈwant to ↘sleep *late*.
g. I just want to relax because I've been so ˈbusy at ↘work *recently*.
h. Could you put your seat forward now, sir? We'll be ↘landing *shortly*.
i. A: Are you ready?
   B: ↘Not *yet*.

但し、文脈によっては、強調されることもある。

・A: Who's that over there? Have you met her?
　B: No, I ˈhaven't met her *be*↘*fore*.
・A: How's the weather?
　B: The temperature is going down, and it's turned very windy. I think it's going to ˈrain *for a* ↘*change*.
・A: Have you finished yet?
　B: ˈNot ↘*yet*.

文末の「時の副詞句」も、通例、二次情報になる。よく出てくる例を挙げよう。

a. A: Did you have a nice weekend, Teresa?
   B: No, I was very tired. I ↘slept *most of the day*.
b. I love to eat out. I ˈeat at ↘restaurants *most of the time*.
c. We went to Disneyland, but my ˈkids were ↘fighting *all the time*.
d. A: What was your weekend like?
   B: Awful. I went to the beach, but it was ˈcold and ↘wet *the whole time*.

e. A: Did you have a good weekend?
   B: Yeah, I had a great weekend. I was out both Friday and Saturday night with friends. But now I'm so tired. I ˈwon't[(1)] do ↘that again *for a while*.

f. A: Where do you want to eat tonight?
   B: ↘Mexican would be ↗nice *for once*. （たまには）

g. A: Have you seen that new show, "Crime City"?
   B: I never watch that stuff. I ˈthink there's ˈtoo much ˈcrime and ↘violence on TV *these days*.

h. A: Sorry to be late.
   B: ˈWhat ↘took you so *long*?

但し、文脈によっては、強調されることもある

・We'll be ˈlanding *in a* ˈ*few* ↘*minutes*. We are collecting the headphones.
・Something's wrong with Rosie lately. She's ˈsad and ˈworried ˈ*all the* ↘*time*.

しかし、final adverbials にもう少し重要度（some degree of importance）を加えたいときには、低い上昇調で言う。その場合、文全体は下降調＋（低）上昇調になる。

i. A: So what's new?
   B: I ˈwent to ↘France | ˈlast ↗week.

j. A: Did anything happen while I was away?
   B: It ↘rained | on ↗Monday. （実際には ↘Monday ↗）

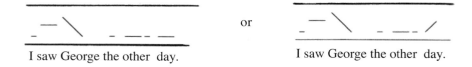

I saw George the other day.　　　or　　　I saw George the other day.

対照的な例を示そう。

(i) We ˈsaw the ˈPrime ↘Minister *yesterday*.

これは標準形で、yesterday は Minister に置かれる核音調の終結部を引き継いで低く発音される。

(ii) We ˈsaw the ˈPrime ↘Minister | ↗*yesterday*. （2つの音調単位）

これは、yesterday が of a certain importance であると見做されている。

課題 7　　Adverbs of time

(iii) We ˈsaw the ⁽¹⁾Prime ˈMinister ↘ *yesterday*.

　これは、prime minister が既に文脈にあり、代名詞に置き換えてもよさそうなケースである。

(iv) We ˈsaw the ˈPrime ↘ Mi<u>ni</u>ster | ↘ *yesterday*.　（2つの音調単位）

　これは、slower and more deliberate tempo で言われる。Prime Minister と yesterday は、共に major information である。

課題 8   Adverbs of place

副詞（句）は、通例、文強勢を受けるが、音調単位の末尾に来る「場所の副詞（句）」は、新情報であっても文強勢を受けないことが多い。例えば、

   a. You've ˈgot a ⁽¹⁾big ↘bruise *on your head*.
   b. You've ˈgot ↘mud *on your hands*.
   c. Hey, ˈhow did you ˈget that ↘oil *on your face*?
   d. She's ˈgot a ↘bee *in her bonnet*. (idiom)
   e. A: Did I do something wrong?
       B: Oh, no. Not at all.
       A: Well, you ˈhave a ⁽¹⁾funny ↘look *on your face*.
   f. She ˈhas a ⁽¹⁾good ↘head *on her shoulders*. (idiom)

同様の強勢配置パターンが、存在文でも見られる。

   g. There's a mos↘quito *on your arm*, Alan.
   h. It's cold; there's ↘snow *in the wind*.
   i. I'm nervous. There's a ↘butterfly *in my stomach*. (idiom)
   j. Waiter, there's a ↘bug *in my soup*.
   k. I bought this sweater yesterday. There's a ↘hole *in the front*.

では、なぜ「場所の副詞（句）」は、文末にあって文強勢を受けないのか。これには語用論が関係する。語用論とは、ことばとその意味を、我々が日常的に行っているコミュニケーションの場面に則して考えていこうとするアプローチである。そのような副詞（句）は、「時の副詞（句）」と同様に、絶えず対話の場面に存在しており、minor information と見なされる。Ladd は、以下の解説をしている。

> Locatives are often deaccented to suggest to the hearer that the location is familiar, close at hand, 'in the context' somehow, to signal that no real 'news' is involved in the specification of the location.
>   *The Structure of Intonational Meaning* (1978:91-92)

また、Jack Windsor Lewis の解説も大いに参考になる。

> A remark like *There's a policeman at the door* might be emphatic enough to be *There's a po\liceman at the \door*, but more usually it's accented as *There's a po\liceman at the door*. *There's someone at the door* would

課題 8　　Adverbs of place

usually be *There's (ˈ)someone at the \door* and virtually never be　***There's *\someone at the door*.

とは言え、場所が重要な情報であるときは、文強勢（核強勢）を受ける。

1. ［警官 A が、走っているバスの横にパトカーを近づけ、バスの運転手 B に大声で叫ぶ］

    A: Hey, I'm a cop. Stop!

    B: What?

    A: There's a ↘bomb | *on your* ↘bus!

2. ［映画 *Free Willy* で、飼育中のオルカ Willy が逃げてしまった］

    There's a ↘hole | *in* ˈWilly's ↘tank!

3. There was a ˈbig ↘earthquake | *in* ↘Chili.

4. One day he ˈsaw a ↘dolphin | *on the* ↘beach.

教室の音声学

課題 9　**You are what you eat.**

　直訳では、you が food と同等になってしまうが、これは、食べものが、私たちの mental and physical conditions に果たす重要性を主張した格言である。いろいろな訳が考えられるが、*Longman Dictionary of Contemporary English* によれば、You will be healthy if the food you eat is healthy. とある。発音上で注意しなければならないのは、機能語 are は、例外的に文強勢を受ける。一方、She is what we call a bookworm. では、is は無強勢である。

　　　You ˈare what you ↘ eat.

この格言から様々な表現が派生する。ある時、*Do you speak American?* というタイトルの DVD を見ていたら、ナレーターが、冒頭で "How we speak to one another defines who we are. We ˈare what we ↘ speak." と言っていた。ちょっと粋なのは、

　　　You ˈare what you ↘ read.

これは、私の街にある大型書店内の壁にある標語にもなっている。更には、

　　　You ˈare what you ↘ wear.

そう言えば、日本の古い諺に、「馬子にも衣装」というのがある。これは、「外形を飾るとりっぱに見える」とか「人は見かけによる」という意味である。Clothes make the man/woman. とか、We are judged by our appearances. と同じ意味である。原型の You are what you eat. から、いっそう派生が進んだ例文を紹介しよう。

　　　You are what you drink. （右写真）
　　　We are what we consume.
　　　You are who you are married to.
　　　You are what car you drive.

このように、いくらでも表現を作ることができるが、その訳し方は、コンテクストによって異なる。私は、退職後、兵庫県にある芦屋聖マルコ教会（Anglican church 英国国教会系）で翻訳の会の支援をしているが、既に翻訳を終え、出版を考えている *You Are Mine: Reflections on Who We Are.*（Alison Webster 著）には、いろいろなバリエーションがあり、訳し方に想像力と工

課題 9　　You are what you eat.

夫がいる。

　　You are what you do.（人となりは、行動を通して表れる）

　　I am what I have lived.（私の人間性は、これまでの人生経験から窺える）

　　I am what I desire.（私の人間性は、私の願望を通して明らかになる）

　　We are what we believe.

　　　（私たちの人となり（人間性）は、何を信じているかに拠っている）

　　We are what we feel and what we remember that we felt, not what we do.

　　　（私たちがどのような人間であるかは、日頃、何を感じ、かつて何を感じた記憶があるかを通して窺われ、日頃の行動／職業からは窺えるものではない）

You are what you do, not what you say you'll do.

課題 10　　**It is quite good.** の意味

　私が昨年に監訳し教文館から出版した翻訳書（原典：*What's the Point of Being a Christian?*）には、以下のくだりがある。

　　ある日、ローマに着いた時、私はアメリカ人のドミニコ会修道士に書類を手渡して、それについて彼のコメントを求めた。彼は、「quite good」と答えた。私は傷ついた。イギリス人には、その表現は「rather bad」の意味である。数日後、彼は、格別においしいパスタ料理について「quite good」と言ったのを聞き、彼がこの表現を私が解釈する意味とは違って使っていることに気づいた。

このような意味の違いについて、『ジーニアス英和大辞典』では、

　　「強勢の置き方は要するに quite を強く発音すれば、被修飾語の意味が弱くなり（「まあまあ」）、逆に弱く発音すれば被修飾語の意味が強くなる」。

しかし、研究社の『新英和大辞典（第6版）』は、「（どちらかと言えば）まあ、多少は、少しは」（英）とあり、発音には全く言及がない。一方、中辞典『レクシス英和辞典』では、「主に英」と「主に米」とに分けて詳しい説明がある。また、多くの英語学習書を出版している Oxford University Press の *Headway Pronunciation* (Intermediate) では、核強勢の位置が意味の区別に関わるとある。

　　Quite can have two different meanings, according to where the main stress (and intonation) is.

　　Type A: It's ˈquite <u>interesting</u>.　（= yes, it's definitely interesting.）

　　Type B: It's <u>quite</u> interesting.　（= but not very interesting.）

　　　　注：main stress とは核強勢のことである（下線部）。強勢の表記は、本書の表記法に変更している。

この解説は、『ジーニアス英和大辞典』にあるものと同じである。しかし、この辞典ではもう1つ大切な様相に関する解説が欠落している。つまり、音調（tones）も、意味の区別に関わっていることが言及されていない。

上記を言い換えると、

　　Type A では、It's ˈquite ↘interesting.

　　Type B では、It's ↘↗quite interesting.

　　　　（注：実際の発音では It's ↘quite interesting↗.）

課題 10　　It is quite good. の意味

私が所属する意見交換ネットワーク SUPRAS（a closed international e-mail list of phoneticians）の会員から寄せられた返信を紹介しよう。

- If a Brit says "The food was ↘↗ QUITE good," that implies very clearly that it wasn't very good. (I don't think an American would say that.) The interpretation of "The food was quite ↘↗ GOOD would suggest some reservation such as ... "but the ↘ DECor wasn't up to much.

  米語では、「食事はとても美味しかったけれども、室内装飾はいまいちだった」

- In American English (my speech, at least), there isn't any difference in meaning between "quite GOOD" and "QUITE good." In fact, "QUITE good" might mean "very, very good". This would simply be a case of emphasis on "quite." The idea of reservation would be expressed not by shifting the tonic, but by the pitch pattern on "good" --- a fall-rise.

- I think there is a dialect difference between British and American usage here. In British English "quite good" is a bit of a put-down. In American English it's positive --- just a tad below "very good". I've run into this problem before with British colleagues, who have misunderstood my use of "quite good," and "quite nice" and have taken these as negative (which was not at all intended).

また、quite+形容詞における意味は、collocation（語の結び付き）と大いに関係があるとも言える。形容詞が「絶対的な意味」── 程度の差が考えられない ── の場合、例えば、dead, exhausted, alone, impossible, enough, right では、quite は「全く、すっかり」の意味になる。これらの形容詞は、a little, very を伴わない。* He is very dead (exhausted, alone...) とは言えない。

課題 11　　会話伝達文のイントネーション

　直接話法で、引用文の箇所を伝達する部分（会話伝達文）は、タイプによって読み方が違うが、ほとんどの人がそのことを認識していないようだ。彼らは、伝達文がどの位置にあっても、独立した音調単位として said, asked, cried, exclaimed などに強勢（しばしば核強勢）を置き、しかも下降調で読む傾向がある。例えば、以下の文中で伝達部をいずれも同じ調子で発音しがちである。

(i)　*She said in a sleepy voice*, "I'm so tired I'm going to bed."

(ii)　"I'm so tired," *she said in a sleepy voice*, "I'm going to bed."

(iii)　"I'm so tired I'm going to bed," *she said in a sleepy voice*.

以下の説明で示すように、文頭伝達文、中間伝達文、文末伝達文の読み方には注意を要する。

(i)　文頭伝達文 She said... は、普通の会話では独立した音調単位を形成せず、said はやや弱い強勢を受け、平坦調（→）で言われる。ただし、朗読の場合、しばしば伝達文は独立した音調単位を形成する。

　　a.　She ˈsaid in a ˈsleepy ↘↗ voice. | "I'm ˈso ˈtired I'm ˈgoing to ↘ bed."

　　b.　He reˈplied to his ↘↗ wife | "Well, I ˈreally don't know."

(ii)　中間伝達文は、会話の中で使用されることはないだろうが、物語の中では頻繁に出てくる。中間伝達文は、通常、独自の音調単位を形成せずに、先行する引用部の音調をそのまま引き継ぐ尾部である。以下の3例の伝達文は、通例、引用部中の核強勢に付加される下降調の終結部を受け継ぐが、時には、末尾で低上昇調になることもある。

　　a.　"Oh, ↘ certainly," said Elizabeth, | "we'll ˈask you ˈno ↘ questions."

　　b.　" ˈLet me ↘ know," said he, | "how ˈmany you'd ↘ like."

　　　　" ˈLet me ↘ know," said he ↗, | "how ˈmany you'd ↘ like."

　　c.　" ˈThis ↘ party," she whispered, | "is a ↘ bore."

　　　　" ˈThis ↘ party," she whispered ↗, | "is a ↘ bore."

・引用文が上昇調の場合、伝達部は、上昇調を受け継ぐ。

　　d.　" ˈOh, you ↘ do, ↗ do you?" said Sam ↗, | "ˈcome ↘ this way, then!"

　　e.　"You ↗ see," he explained ↗, | "these ˈsnakes are ⁽¹⁾ quite ↘ tame."

　　f.　" ˈAll ↗ right," he answered ↗. | "ˈCome ↘ with me, and I'll ↘ show you."

課題11　会話伝達文のイントネーション

　　上記の例にもあるように、中間伝達文の動詞と主語の語順が入れ替わることもある。

(iii) 文末伝達文は、会話中では頻度が低いが、朗読では、この位置が普通である。特に、伝達文が比較的長い場合には後置されることが多い。また、文末伝達文は、通常、先行する引用文のイントネーションを受け継ぐ。

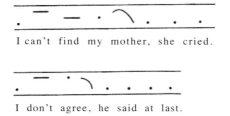

伝達文が上昇調になる例：

以下のような、解説付きの表記もある。

$com^{ing,}\ she\ ask^{ed}$
Are you　　　　　　　　　　　　（high-rise with nucleus on *com-*）

out
Get　　　　　　　　　　　　　　（fall with nucleus on *out*）
of here, he yelled

$think$
I don't
so, he sa^{id}　（fall-rise with nucleus on *think*）

Ladd, R. *The Structure of Intonational Meaning* (1980:164)

課題 12　　Excuse ME. と Excuse YOU.

(1) ある時、教授会で私の隣に座っていたカナダ人教員が、軽くくしゃみをした。その時、彼女は、Excuse me. と呟いた。これを、もう少し詳しい表記をすると、下降調 Exˈcuse ↘ me. となる。他に下降・上昇調で言われる Exˈcuse ↘↗ me. もある。ところが、これとは全く逆の意味になる Excuse me. もある。誰かから無礼なことをされて抗議するときにも使われる。但し、イントネーションは上昇・下降調である。この音調は、基本的には下降調と似ているが、stronger feeling を伝える。例えば、Exˈcuse ↘ me. に対して Exˈcuse ↗↘ me. と表す。

　　　　注：「下降調」の意味は、核強勢のところで声が急に下降するというのではなく、多くの場合、その直前に声が核音節に向かっていったん上昇し、後に下降するという意味である。また、「上昇・下降調」は、更に高く上昇し、それから下降に転じるということである。

John Wells の *English Intonation* (2006:219) には、

　(i)　Exˇcuse me.　（下降・上昇調）

　(ii)　Ex ˈcuse ˆme.　（上昇・下降調）

Pattern (i) is the way person A might politely ask person B to move so that he, A, could get past. Pattern (ii) is the way B might ironically react if A pushed in front of her without saying anything…The tone meaning of the rise-fall is a challenge.

無礼に対する抗議とは、例えば、自分を押しのけて通ろうとした人に向かって言うときの表現である。私は、最近、映画の中で、これと似た状況で発せられる Excuse me. を聞いた。ある女性が、ドアーに背を向け立っていると、突然、それが開き、男性が現れ、彼女は突き飛ばされそうになった。彼女は、足早に立ち去っていく男の後ろ姿に向かって、Exˈcuse ↗↘ me. と叫んだ。ところで、Exˈcuse ↘ you. も同じ意味で言われる。道路を歩いている男性が、反対側から来る男性とすれ違うときに互いの肩が衝突したときに、何もなかったかのように歩き去る後ろ姿に向かって、彼は Exˈcuse ↘ you. と言った。また、相手が道を塞いでいたりして通れない時など、ムカッとなり Excuse you. と言ったりする。

　　昔、私のホームステイ先で、ゴールデンレトリーバーの愛犬が fart を

課題 12　Excuse ME. と Excuse YOU.

した。その時、男の子が、犬に向かって、Ex¹cuse ↘you. と言うのを聞いたことがある。インターネットに、次のような留学体験記があった。
「ある晩の御飯時、我が家でパーティをしていると、お姉さんが料理をテーブルまで運んできてくれました。ソファーに座って喋っていた男の子が「うわぁーうまそー！」と料理に手をつけようとした時、お姉さんが男の子の手をバシッとはたきながら一言。Excuse you! アメリカ人の旦那に聞いたのですが、身内にはよく使いますが、他人には腹立つ時に使うそうです」。

(2) I beg your pardon. について
　この表現は、短縮形の Pardon? と共に、反復を求める表現として、学習段階の早い時期で学ぶ。文字通りの意味は、自分の過失や無礼に対して謝罪することである。実は、謝罪も、反復を求める場合と同様に、上昇調で発せられることがある。では、両者の違いはどこにあるのだろうか。
　D. Jones, *English Phonetics* (9ᵗʰ edition,1960:306) と P. Christopher, *An English Phonetics Course* (1956:195) によれば、

(i)　謝罪のイントネーション：
　A: Don't interrupt me.
　B: I ↘beg your ↗pardon. I thought you'd finished.

　　I beg your pardon
　　　(as an apology)

　I から beg にかけて、いったん声のピッチが大きく上昇して、その後は下降し最終的に -don で上昇する。末尾で上昇するのは politeness を伝えるためである。また、更に真摯な謝罪を表わすには、I do beg your pardon. や I do apologize. があり、do でいったんピッチが上昇する。

(ii)　反復を乞うイントネーション：
　　(requesting repetition
　　 of something
　　 previously said)

　飛行機の離陸の軌跡のように、イントネーションは文頭の I を起点にして比較的滑らかに上昇していく。

(iii) 反駁（抗議）のイントネーション：
　この表現にはもう 1 つの意味がある。例えば、映画を観ているときに以下

のセリフを聞いた。
- a. A: You're an old fool.
   B: ‾I ↗ beg your pardon!
- b. A: (pointing to B) I don't trust that woman.
   B: ‾I ↗ beg your pardon!
   C: (to A) Samantha, you owe Miss Warbell an apology.
- c. A: Nora, the ladies and I would like you to play the piano.
   B: No.
   A: ‾I ↘↗ beg your pardon!　　注：Nora は 5 歳の子供

c. は more emphatic type である（実際には ‾I ↘ beg your pardon ↗.）

I beg your pardon?

　　　　　　　　　　　　安部勇『日英イントネーション法』（1972:66）

文脈から推測できるように、この場合の I beg your pardon! は謝罪とは正反対の意味があり、How dare you say that! とか、How rude you are to say that! と言い換えができる（used to show that you strongly disagree or that you are _angry_ about something that someone has said.

(3) 社交辞令としての I'm sorry.

New Horizon 2（旧版）には、4 回も I'm sorry. が出てくる。

　　‾I'm ↗ sorry.

この表現は、最初に I を高く言ってから少し下降し、sorry で軽く上昇する。ちょっとした社交上の間違いであったり、相手の期待に応えられないときに使われる。末尾が低く上昇する。短縮形 ↘Sorry ↗. でも低上昇になる。

- A: Can you help me?
- B: ‾I'm ↗ sorry. I can't. I'm busy now.

なお、I に付されている横棒の記号は、高前頭部（high prehead）を示す。詳細は、課題 25 を参照されたい。

課題 13　　You are a dark horse!

もし You are a dark horse! と言われたら困惑するだろう。日本語のダークホースの意味で解釈するとチンプンカンプンになる。dark horse は、本来、競馬で実力不明の馬。また、予想外の活躍をして番狂わせを演じるかもしれない馬または競争相手も dark horse である。しかし、そのような意味で以下の対話を見ると、困惑するだろう。

a. Wife: The Joneses have got a new car.
   Husband: Have they, indeed? What model is it, dear?
   Wife: Oh, I don't know. It's a pale blue.
   Husband: Well, well, <u>Old Ted is a dark horse</u>. I was only talking cars with him the other night.
   Wife: And he didn't mention it?
   Husband: Not a word.

b. A: I've just got engaged to Sheila.
   B: Well! <u>You are a dark horse.</u> I didn't know you were courting her.

ここではダークホースは、自分についてあまり語らない人（a person who keeps his or her interests and ideas secret）のことである。話者は、驚いている。従って、その時のイントネーションがユニークである。標準型の You're a ˈdark ↘horse. ではなく、You ↘are a dark horse. と言う。

実は、この 2 例は、10 年前に、私が John Wellsにメールを送り、確認をした内容の一部である。Wellsは、私への返信の代わりに、彼の phonetic blog (Monday, 14 September 2009) に記事を掲載した。その一部を紹介しよう。

Tami Date asked for my comments on the accent pattern of the underlined parts below. (中略) My immediate reaction was to suggest that 'be a dark horse' is an idiom with a fixed pattern. A *dark horse* is someone who is not well known and who surprises people by winning a competition; hence, someone who acts secretively to surprise people... What we want is an <u>accented verb **to be** followed by lexical material that is new in context but unaccented.</u>

注：'be a dark horse' は、be が核強勢を受けることを示す。また、lexical material は、内容語と同じ意味である。下線は伊達が追加

上記の例では、新情報の内容語 dark と horse が文アクセントを受けていない。これは、「異常事態」である。核強勢を受け、最も強調して発音される語 —— is と are —— は、それぞれ is not と are not との対比ではない。

 Cf. A: It's cold today.
   B: No, it isn't.
   A: It ↘is cold, very cold. （対比）

この異常さが、文全体の意味を強調している。つまり、感情移入（emotionally colored）がある。

 In gushing speech the intonation turn can fall on almost any word of the sentence. The more unusual an intonation, the greater its emotional value.
  Schubiger, *The Role of Intonation in Spoken English* (1935:44)
   注：gushing は、「感情吐露を伴った（emotional）」の意味で、intonation turn は核音調のことである。

例えば、驚きの気持が込められているケースがある。
子どもをほめるとき、
 c. You ↘are a clever boy/girl!
不器用な人に向かって、
 d. Oh, you ↘are clumsy!
見事な手腕を発揮するする人に向かって、
 e. You ↘are a wonder!
思いがけないところで知人と遭遇し、
 f. Well, ˈthis ↘is a surprise!

感情移入と言えば、exclamation である。以下の平叙文は感嘆文と同等の意味になる。
 g. The ˈweather ↘is hot today!
 h. ˈThat ↘would be a good idea.
 i. We ↘did have fun.
 j. Oh, you ↘do look smart!
 k. Oh, she ↘did seem sad!
 l. We ↘have enjoyed ourselves.

課題 13　You are a dark horse!

- m. A: Let me introduce you to our new neighbor.
  B: ⌐How ↘do you do?

そのほか、insistence や challenge，suspicion などの気持ちもある。

- n. Keep quiet! ⌐This ↘is a hospital.
- o. ⌐What ↘are you doing?
- p. Hey, ⌐where ↘are you going at this late hour?
- q. ［クリスマスツリーの片づけが延び延びになっている］
  Wife: Darling George...
  Husband: Yes?
  Wife: I know that you've been busy, but it ↘is February.

課題 14　　　相手の反応を窺うイントネーション

　友人たちどうしの雑談の最中に、ある土地の話、例えば、長崎の話が出たとしよう。すかさず誰かが、"Oh, my mother was born in Nagasaki." と相槌を打つ。この文は、どのようなイントネーションで発せられるだろうか。
　a.　?Oh, my ˈmother was ↘born in Nagasaki.
一見すると、これは妥当な言い方に思える。しかし、ネーティブスピーカーは、多分、そのようには言わずに、次のように言うだろう。
　b.　Oh, my ↘mother was born in Naga ↗saki.
両者には、談話上の違いがある。a. の下降調のイントネーションは、やや事務的に（matter-of-factly）聞こえる。換言すれば、ややそっけない印象を与える。しかも、my mother が既知情報の扱いになっている。b. では、born は初出の内容語であるにもかかわらず強勢が抑制される。実は、「初出の名詞」と「初出の動詞」が、同じ文中で用いられるとき、後者の強勢が抑制される。また、下降調は、mother が new and major information であることを伝えるために用いられ、（低）上昇調は、Nagasaki が話し手と聞き手の間に共有された副次情報（minor information）であるのを示す。では、なぜ話し手は、in Nagasaki を簡略して、単に there と言わないのだろうか。端的に言えば、そこにいわば未練があるからである。2 度目ではあるが、Nagasaki に二次的な重要度（some less important but not completely negligible idea）を与え、そのまま繰り返している。更には、話し手は、下降調＋上昇調の「複合音調（complex tone）」を通して、話題に関心があるというシグナルを送り、この情報をきっかけにして会話が新たな展開をすることを期待している。つまり、相手の反応を窺っている。"Come on — let's talk about it."　このような複合音調は、日本語には存在しないが、英語ではしばしば見られる。
　c.　A: I'd like to go to Australia someday.
　　　B: Really? My ↘sister lives in Aust ↗ralia.
これについて文献には次のような解説がある。

　Repeating the words *in Australia* at the end of the sentence means: "Come on — let's talk about it." This way we can keep the subject open.
　　　　　　　　　　　　　　　Thompson, *Intonation Practice* (1981:54)

以下も、冒頭の例 b と類似したケースである。

課題 14　相手の反応を窺うイントネーション

d.　A: I'm going to Sheffield tomorrow.
　　B: Really? My ↘mother came from ↗Sheffield.

これについて文献には次のような解説がある。

[M]other, which is new, is clearly more important than *Sheffield*, which has been already mentioned, and <u>the way is open for the conversation to continue</u>. So in general, we can say that the Fall is used to mark the most important idea in a plain statement, while Low Rise indicates <u>some less important but not completely negligible idea</u> that follows the main idea, and in addition we can say that the Low Rise constitutes **an appeal to the listener** and invites him to say more about the subject of the previous conversation.

　　　　O'Connor & Arnold, *Intonation of Colloquial English* (1973:83-4)

e.　A: How's it going, Amy?
　　B: All right. I'm writing a research paper on Leonardo da Vinci, so I've been spending a lot of time in the library.
　　A: Oh yeah, ↘I know ↗him. Isn't he that guy who painted the *Mona Lisa*?
　　B: That's right. He also did a lot of other great paintings.

ここでも、"Come on — let's talk about it." This way we can keep the subject open. と言える。

驚いたことに、旧版の中学検定教科書 1 年生 *New Horizon* 1 にも、早々と以下の場面がある。

　　↘I know ↗her.　（準拠 CD に基づく）

また、I re ↘member ↗you. も、同じニューアンスである。一方、I ↘know her. は、素っ気ない印象を与える。しかし、このような教材は、自然で colloquial であるとは言え、入門期の英語教育を無視している。教員用の指導書には、解説どころか、言及すらもない。

63

下降調＋上昇調は英語独特なものであり、他の言語では極めて稀であると言われている。日本の英語教育では、この音調は話題になっていないように思われるが、英語らしいインとネーションを身に付けるには欠かすことができないものである。Wells と Kingdon は次のように言う。

・Students of EFL may need to spend time practicing the leading fall-rise. It is a tone very characteristic of mainstream English (RP and GA), yet rare or absent in most other languages.

English Intonation (2006:70)

・Tone III (i.e. fall-rise) is used more extensively in English than in most other languages, and the failure to use it is one of the foreign student's most frequent mistakes in English intonation. In Britain the incidence of Tone III in conversation is about 30 per cent of the total of kinetic tones, but in America its rate of occurrence must be even higher,...

The Groundwork of English Intonation (1958:84)

課題 15　　**I don't want a ticket.**

　私は、GDM英語教授法研究会主催のワークショップで発音指導法を担当している。以下は、演習用の資料の一つである。

[The conductor (A) comes around to the passenger (B).]

A: Tickets.

B: No, thanks.

A: (In surprise) Pardon?

B: I don't want a ticket, thank you.

A: I'm not selling tickets, sir.

B: No?

A: No, I want to see your ticket.

B: Oh, I haven't got a ticket.

A: You haven't got a ticket?

B: No, I never buy a ticket.

A: Why not?

B: Well, they're very expensive, you know.

　実は、参加者のほぼ全員が、下線の否定文において、don't, not, haven't, never を特に強調して発音する ── つまり、そこに核強勢を置く ── 傾向が顕著であった。

　　＊ I ↘don't want a ticket.

　　＊ I'm ↘not selling tickets.

　　＊ I ↘haven't got a ticket.

　　＊ I ↘never buy a ticket.

　　　　　注：星印（asterisk）は、「不適」を表す

私が、参加者にこのようなイントネーションは、文脈を反映していないことを指摘すると、最初は、納得しないそぶりだった。だって、「欲しくない」、「もっていない」、「売っていない」、「買わない」という意味だから、否定語を強く言うべきではないですか、という返答があった。いきなり、音声学理論を振りかざすと失礼になるので、私は、次の対話を紹介して、最も強調して発音する語を尋ねた。

(1) A: Please sign your name here.

　　B: Sorry, I don't have a pen. May I borrow one?

やはり、I ↘don't have a pen. と言う。次に、別の対話を紹介した。

(2) X: Please sign your name here. Do you have a pen?
     Y: No, I don't have a pen. May I borrow one?

この場合も I ↘don't have a pen. と言う。

ようやく、(1) と (2) では、コンテクストが違うのに、I don't have a pen. が同じイントネーションになるというのは変だと感じ始め、当惑の表情を見せる。そこで、簡単な「種明かし」をした後、二人の native speakers（英と米）のモデルを聞いてもらった。そうすると、「目から鱗」のような反応をする人がいた。この後は、音声学上の強勢配置規則を説明した。正しい言い方は、

　　I 'don't ↘want a ticket.
　　I'm 'not ↘selling tickets.
　　I 'haven't ↘got a ticket.
　　I 'never ↘buy a ticket.

核配置に適切な場所を選択する方法は、音調単位の末尾から始め、1 語ずつ前へ（左へ）さかのぼっていくことである。上記の否定文では、ticket は既知情報であるので、核強勢を受ける資格はない。だから、前へ（左へ）移動する。もし途中に機能語があれば、それを無視する。さかのぼっていく際に、「最初に出合う」内容語が、核強勢を受ける最有力候補になる。I ↘don't want a ticket. で、don't を最も強調して言う（核強勢を置く）ことが不適切である理由は、最初に出合う内容語 want を無視して ── それを飛び越えて ── いるからである。このように、核強勢の配置の規則は、実に単純である。要は、話者の意図が文を否定することであっても、否定語・否定表現の後に位置する新情報の内容語を無視してはいけない。

　ただし、存在文の場合には、「前へ（左へ）」遡っていくやり方は通用しない。語順が S+V ではなく、V+S となるからである。

　　a. I wanted some cheese, but there ↘was no cheese.
　　b. A: What did you think of the garden? Were the flowers any good?
　　　 B: There ↘were no flowers there.
　　c. A: If something's right, how can it be a waste of time?
　　　 B: There ↘is no right or wrong. There's only opinion.
　　d. A: Well, she'll do better next time.
　　　 B: There 'won't ↘be any next time.

課題 16　　I left it somewhere.

かつて、「センター試験」に次のような出題があった。

　Ted: Where did I put it?
　Kei: What are you looking for?
　Ted: (1) I can't find my wallet. Oh, no, maybe (2) I left it somewhere.
　Kei: Gee, that's too bad. Where were you last?
　Ted: Let's see... I went to the bookshop and bought a magazine.
　（以下は省略）

(1) と (2) では、どの語が最も強調して発音されるか、換言すれば、どの語が核強勢を受けるかという問題である。大半の受験生は、somewhere を選ぶであろう。しかし、正解は、left が核強勢を受ける。文末の somewhere は文強勢を受けない。somewhere は、left に置かれる下降調の終結部を引き継ぎ、低い key で（余韻のように）発音される。日本語の言語感覚に合わないと感じる人が多いだろう。

　そもそも、不定副詞 somewhere や不定代名詞 something, somebody は、言語環境によって、文強勢を受けたり、受けなかったりする。特に、somewhere は、sentence-final position にある時は、一般の「時の副詞」（now, today, tonight, tomorrow, the other day など）と同様に、文強勢を受けない。また、不定代名詞も動詞や形容詞の目的語となる場合には、文強勢を受けない。従って、核強勢も受けない。課題 35 を参照。

　　　　　↘Do something.
　　　　　I ˈmet someone at the ↘party.
　　　　　Flusk, Flusk. That's a curious name. It seems to ring a ↘bell somewhere.
　　　　　　　　　　　　　　　　　　　　　　（どこかで聞き覚えがある）
　　　　cf. There's ˈsomebody at the ↘door.
　　　　　　ˈSomething is ↘wrong with him.
　　　　　　He's ↘somewhere. (essential complement)　　課題 59 参照。

以前、上記のセンター試験問題について、Wells にメールを送ったことがあった。以下のような返信があった。

　In my view, a tonic on **somewhere** in (2) is not possible. **Somewhere** would surely be treated as an empty word, like **things**, **one**, **people**, **place**. It would be possible to accent final *somewhere*, but only in a context such as Ted: I've looked ↘EVerywhere! I must have left it ↘↗SOMEwhere, where there is an implied contrast with ***nowhere***.

   注：tonic は、nucleus stress（核強勢）と同義である。

往年の名曲『虹の彼方に』*Somewhere Over The Rainbow* にも somewhere が出てくるが、この場合は、non-final position にあるので文強勢を受ける。従って、

 ˈSomewhere ˈover the ↗rainbow

 ˈWay up ↗high

 And the ˈdreams that you ↘dreamed of

 ˈOnce in a ↘lullaby

ところで get somewhere という慣用表現がある。make progress と同義である。ここでも somewhere は文強勢を受けない。

 a. Now we're getting somewhere. （ようやく見通しがついてきた）

 b. At last | I ˈfelt we were getting somewhere.

しかし、逆の意味をもつ not get anywhere では anywhere が文強勢（しばしば核強勢）を受ける。

 c. Comˈplaining ˈwon't [l]get you anywhere. （何の得にもならない）

 d. Being ˈstubborn ˈwon't [l]get you anywhere.

 e. You ˈwon't [l]get anywhere | without qualifications.

課題 17　　新情報 vs. 既知情報

音調単位では、new information は文強勢を受け、'given' information は文強勢を受けない。ここで言う 'given' は「既知の」の意味で、「当事者間で了解されている（共有されている）」ことである。例えば、

A: ˈHow about ˈgoing there on ↘ˈfoot?
B: OK. I ↘like walking.

ここでは、walking は初出の内容語であるが文強勢を受けない。なぜならば、既知内容だからである。

　　　　* I ˈlike ↘walking.　　（不適）

以下は、10年前のセンター試験で出題された問題である。

　次の会話の下線部 (1) ～ (4) について、それぞれ下の問い（問1～4）に示された①～④の中から、最も強調して発音されるものを一つずつ選べ。

《状況》Maya は、日本に来てまもない留学生の Jeff と買い物に出かける。

Maya:　Here comes our train. It's not too crowded.
Jeff:　　Do the trains (1)get any worse than this?
Maya:　Oh, yes. During the morning rush hour, (2)they're twice as bad.
Jeff:　　I can't imagine a train being more crowded than this. Where I'm from, (3)we can always get a seat.
Maya:　You were lucky, but you'll have to get used to the crowds here. How do you get to school? Do you take a train?
Jeff:　　No, (4)I walk to school.

問1　① get　　② any　　③ worse　　④ than
問2　① they're　② twice　③ as　　　④ bad
問3　① we　　② can　　③ always　　④ get
問4　① I　　　② walk　　③ to　　　　④ school

率直に言って、問1と問3には、正解の「揺れ」を回避する出題者の意図が明らかである。もし問1で this が選択肢に入っておれば、それが正解になる可能性がある。そうであっても、私の直感では、③ worse が核強勢を受けるのが妥当である。なぜならば、this は 'given'（= shared information, common ground）であるからである。今更、this を強調する必要はない。しかし、人によっては、this に焦点を置く可能性は排除できない。もし this が選

択肢の一つだったら、センター試験事務局に抗議の電話が殺到しただろう。問2では、bad は初出の内容語であるけれども、既に worse と言われているので、概念的には 'given' である。従って、核強勢を受ける next candidate は、② twice である。核強勢の位置を考える手順は、音調単位の末尾から始め、1語ずつ順番に考え、音調単位の初めに向かって左へ進んで行く。もし文強勢を受けない語 — 'given' — があれば、その次の内容語が核強勢を受ける候補になる。上記の場合、bad は 'given' なので、左に進み、twice に行き当たる。問3は、奇問である。We can always get a seat. は、本来、seat が核強勢を受ける候補であるにもかかわらず、それが選択肢に入っていない。もし動詞 get を強調する — 核強勢を置く — と、他の動詞との対比になる。例えば、find, take などとの対比になる。日本人学習者の悪癖は、名詞よりも動詞を重要視することである。例えば、

 A: So where did you go in your free time?
  B: *I ↘visited the museum.（不適）
  X: You're angry with your brother. What did he do?
  Y: *He ↘broke my smartphone.（不適）

まるで passed by the museum とか、dropped my smartphone との対比の印象を与える。従って、④ get はあり得ない。正解は、③ always であろう。蛇足になるが、対話文中の Where I'm from では、in MY country (city) の意味であるので、Where ↘↗I'm from というイントネーションになる。

 もっとも物議を呼んだのは、1998年の出題であった。

 A: Are you free after work today? I was hoping we could do something together.
 B: Well, sure, <u>but aren't you going to the health club</u>? I thought you went there every day.
  ① but ② going ③ health ④ club

センターの発表では、正解は③であった。試験の翌日に、私は海外の研究者たち（a closed international e-mail list）に、一斉配信し、どの語に音調核を置くのが妥当と考えるかと問うた。様々な意見が発信された。その中には、このような artificial dialogue では話者の心理は推し量れないから、正解は1つに絞れないという強硬な意見が出た。また、文脈から判断すると、A が health club に通っていることは shared information であるから、aren't が正解ではな

課題 17　新情報 vs. 既知情報

いか。また health club は、上昇調の文の末尾にあり、club が最も高い pitch で発音され目立つので、それが最も強調されていると言えるのでないか（課題 33 参照）。当時、筆者の勤務大学の native speaker 教員にも答えてもらった。5 名の中、3 名が aren't を最も強調して発音するとのことであった。他の 2 人は正解とされる health を選んだ。なお、複合語は、前の要素に強勢があるとされている。ˈbus stop, ˈkitchen knife, ˈtea time

　先ほど「話者の心理は推し量れないから、正解は 1 つに絞れないという強硬な意見」と言ったが、実は、以下のような裏付けがある。文中のどの語が核強勢を受けるかについては一般的な合意があるものの、それを決めるのは話者自身である。つまり、話者の communicative intentions が、文中のどの語に文強勢（しばしば核強勢）を置くかの決め手となる。イントネーションの研究では巨星的存在の Dwight Bolinger というアメリカ人言語学者がいた。数ある著書の中で *Intonation And Its Parts*（1986）と *Intonation and Its Uses*（1989）は研究者には必携の書である。彼のコメント（1989:142）は、誠に意義深い。

> What counts is... how the speaker feels about what he is saying. A speaker may override the semantic importance of the words in his utterance, and even the 'given'/new status of those words, for a particular communicative effect. Thus he may choose to focus on a 'given' (repeated) word.

つまり、話者は、発言の効果を狙って、既知項目に焦点を当てる —— 核強勢を置く —— ことがある。海外のスシ人気の今日では、もう好例とは言えなくなってしまったが、Bolinger（1986:90）には、次の対照例がある。

(1) Raw fish is good for you, but after all, ˈwho ↘ *likes it*?
(2) Raw fish is good for you, but after all, ˈwho ˈlikes ⁽ˈ⁾raw ↘ *fish*?
(3) Raw fish is good for you, but after all、ˈwho ˈlikes ↘ *that*?

(1) は、特別な感情・態度を伴わない matter-of-fact な言い方である。それに対して (2) は、嫌悪感が込められている。sushi を食べる人が増えてきているとはいえ「生魚なんて」嫌だよ。話者がわざわざ raw fish を反復しているのは for a particular communicative effect を意図しているからである。(3) は、(2) と同じ感情で「そんなもの」御免だよというニュアンスがある。

以下も、既知（旧）情報が、核強勢を受けている例である。

　a.　A: ［辛い食べ物を口に入れ］It's very hot!

B: Oh, Jim, *it's ˈnot ↘ hot*. It's invigorating.

A: I'm beginning to see stars. Could you pass me the water, please?

b. Mother: And they lived happily ever after.

   Child: And then what?

   Mother: That's all.

   Child: No, read more.

   Mother: Well, *there's ˈno more to ↘ read*, sweetheart.

c. A: You know, this *sushi* tastes so good you don't even think of it as raw fish.

   B: (in surprise) *I'm ˈeating ⁽¹⁾raw ↗ fish?*

d. A: Sorry, I'm on a diet.

   B: But, if you eat chocolate, *ˈhow can you be on a ↘ diet?*

e. A: What did the doctor say?

   B: That he was poisoned.

   A: Poisoned? Poisoned? *ˈWhat ⁽¹⁾kind of ↘ poison?*

f. A: Tell me about Kaitlin Costello.

   B: *There's ˈnothing to ↘ tell*.

g. A: I *ˈlike what you're ↘ wearing*.

   B: Thanks.

   A: And *I ˈlove the ˈway you ↘ wear it*.

h. A: Why're you upset?

   B: Well, *it's ˈnot what he ↘↗ said; but the ˈway he ↘ said it*.

i. Tony Blair warned radical Muslims, "*Our ↘ tolerance | is ˈpart of what ˈmakes ˈBritain ↘ Britain*. Conform to it; or don't come here. We don't want hate-mongers, whatever their race, religion or creed.

   （寛容は英国を今日の英国にしている）

課題 18　　慣用的表現 I know. と I don't know.

《 *I know.* について 》

(1) 相手の発言に同調・同意したりする場合、

 a. A: Look. There's Tom Cruise.

   B: Shh, I ↘know.

 b. A: We have to talk about it, Bill.

   B: Yeah, I ↘know.

(2) 何かを思いついたり、気づいた場合

 Peter: And who do you work for, Anna?

 Anna: I work for AJ dot com.

 Peter: Ah, ↘I ↗know. Do you sell computers?

 Anna: Yes, we do.

John Wells から、以下の解説があった。

> Yes, this is an intonation idiom, when "I know" is used to say that you have suddenly had an idea or suddenly thought of a solution to a problem. It has two nuclear accents, fall plus rise.　(2003.5.28)

(3) 相手を安心させたり (for reassurance)、自分が既に認識していることを相手からくどくどと聞かされて、それを制止するためのイントネーションは、以下のようになる。

 a. A: Dave, that's crazy.

   B: I ↘know, I ↘know. I should have had the car checked

 b. A: Look at the time. You've got to hurry.

   B: I ↗know. (for reassurance)

《 *I don't know.* について 》

Longman Dictionary of Cotemporary English には、つぎの表記がある。

 A: I couldn't live there.　（仮定法）

 B: Oh, I don't know. It might not be so bad.

この辞書の定義には "used to show that you disagree slightly with what has just been said" とある。下線部は、I don't know whether or not I can agree with you. の短縮形であるが、日本語相当句では「さあ、どうですかね」となる

だろう。軽い上昇調 ── 低上昇調 ── で言えば、決めつける印象を与えず、語調が柔らかくなる。つまり、相手の意見に対して、polite disagreement を表している。従って、Wells は、demurring という表題の phonetic blog (26 October 2011) の中で、次のように述べている。

>What intonation would be appropriate for *I don't know* in this sense? I think it has to be a rise.
>
>I ˈdon't /know. or
>
>\Oh ǀ, I ˈdon't /know.

他の意味のイントネーションの例を挙げよう。

 a. A: You've done a good job. （車の修理のこと）

  B: Oh, ↘↗ I don't know. You'd have done it just as well.

 b. A: When will Tom be back?

  B: ↘↗ I don't know. Why not ask him?

ここでは、核強勢が主語の I に来ている。これは、「他の人のことはともかく私は」という**対比**を意味する。下降調の核強勢が I で始まり、以降は低上昇調に転じ、それが文末まで及ぶ。他の表記で示すと \I don't know ↗. となる（know には文強勢はない）。この対比用法の例 a. を Wells に送ったら、返信があった。

>Thanks. This intonation is not a demurral ── not a polite disagreement ── but a genuine disclaiming of knowledge. It has a contrastive focus on "I", with the implication that other people may know about mechanical things, but not the speaker.

《 *I see.* について 》

(1) 了解（I understand, I follow）という意味の場合

 A: Good afternoon. May I help you?

 B: No, thanks. I'm just looking.

 A: I ↘ see. Please call me if you need any help.

(2) 何かが理解でき始めたり、または、納得する場合

 a. A: Excuse me. Where's the beach?

  B: Oh, it's on the opposite side of the lake. It's between the lake and the trees at the back of the park.

  A: *Oh,* ↘ I ↗ see.

課題 18　　慣用的表現 I know. と I don't know.

  b. A: Excuse me, but how can I get to downtown New York?
     B: You can take either a bus or a taxi.
     A: ↘I ↗see.

(3) 失望の感情を表す場合

    Oh, I ↘see...　　（see を伸ばし加減で言う）

課題 19　　句動詞の強勢

　今回は、英語のプロソディの中でも特に複雑な様相を見せる句動詞（two-word verbs）の強勢を論じる。句動詞とは、動詞と副詞（±前置詞）とが組み合わさり、動詞と同様の働きをする語群のことである。

　句動詞は、文脈や韻律関係によって強勢の置き方が自在に変化するので体系的な知識が必要である。句動詞は基本的には two-stress verbs であるが、実際の発話では周囲の韻律的状況の影響を受けて、いくつかの異なったストレス・パターンになる。これらの変異は、大体において予測できるものである。

(1) 句動詞の最も単純な形態は、音調単位がそれだけで終わっていたり、あるいは句動詞が休止（pause）の直前に来る場合である。その際は、英語特有の stress-timed rhythm を反映して動詞が幾分弱くなる。

　　　　ˌstand ˈup; ˌcome ˈin; ˌgo ˈhome; ˌsit ˈdown, etc.

　　　　Whát did you run óver?

　　　　Whát did you spéak about?　　（about は前置詞）

　句動詞は two-stress verbs でありながら、自然なスピードの発音では2つのストレス間に優劣関係が生じる。その理由は、英語では強勢音節の衝突（stress clash）を避けようとし、どちらかを弱めようとするからである。その犠牲になるのは、動詞である。なぜなら、副詞が音調単位の末尾に位置しているため、文末焦点（end focus）を受けるからである。実際、映画のスクリーン・プレイなどには C'mon や C'min という表記があることから come が弱められていることが分る。しかし、*Come on *in や *Come on *up では、副詞 on が弱勢となり全体の好律性（強・弱・強）が保たれるので come は弱められることはない。（注：記号 * は、文強勢のある語を示す。）句動詞以外でも、*A *B *C (slower tempo) ⇒ *A B *C (faster); *big *bad *wolf (slower tempo) ⇒ *big bad *wolf (faster) などのように強勢音節が3つ並ぶと中間のものが強勢を失う。これは、**the rule of three**（「3連規則」）と呼ばれる。

(2) 句動詞の直後に3つめの強勢音節が来る場合は、逆に副詞のほうが弱くなる。例えば、

　　a.　They *got along *WELL.　　cf. *How did they *get a*LONG?

課題 19　　句動詞の強勢

  b.　He *gave in *FInally.　　　cf. *FInally he gave *IN.

  c.　She *called in *SICK.

(3) 句動詞＋名詞目的語では、発話のスピードによって、動詞と副詞におけるストレスの優劣関係が変化する。まず、比較対照となる 2 文を提示しよう。

  a.　(i)　He looked up the hill.　（丘の上の方を見上げた）

    (ii) He looked up the word.　（語の意味を調べた）

up は、前者では前置詞であり、後者では副詞である。ゆっくりとした発音の phrasing（句の区切り）は、それぞれ look + up the hill と look up + the word である。このような短い文は、通常、1 つの音調単位で発音され、その際に意味の決定に大きく関与するのはストレスである。「丘の上の方を見上げた」では up はストレスを受けないのに対して、「(辞書で) 語の意味を調べた」では、up はストレスを受ける。ここで問題となるのは、動詞と副詞とのストレスの優劣関係である。どちらが他方よりも強いのか。原則的には、副詞のストレスのほうが強い。以下の各ペアーの (ii) についても同じことが言える。

  a.　(i)　He *turned off the *ROAD.　（その道から離れた）

    (ii) He *turned *off the *RAdio.

  b　(i)　He *looked over the *FENCE.　（垣根越しに見た）

    (ii) He *looked *over the *PROject.

しかし、このようなストレス配分は、比較的 slower tempo で発音される場合に起こるのであって、実際の natural normal speed では、リズム原理である the rule of three の影響を受けて、中間の強勢が抑制される。

ほかにも、自然な（速い）スピードでは、

  He *looked up the *WORD.

  He *picked up *SPEED.　（スピードを上げた）

  I've *put away the *BOOKS.　（本をかたづけた）

  He's *cleaned out his *DESK.　（机の中のものをかたづけた）

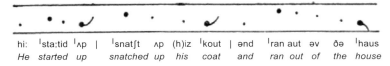

Jones, The Pronunciation of English (1956:287)

(4) 動詞の前に just や do のような強勢音節の語が来る場合、動詞のほうが強

勢を失う。

 He's *just cleaned *out his *DESK.

 I *just came *up here to change my SHOES.

 *Do come *in and have a SEAT.

 Did *Jim get *IN yet?

(5) 分離型の句動詞を伴う文の場合では、強勢を受ける初出の名詞の直後にある副詞は強勢を受けない。やはり、強勢の衝突を避けるためである。ここからは、本来の表記法に戻ることにする。

 He ˈput his ˈhat on.

 He ˈtook his ˈshoes off.

しかし、名詞が既に文脈に存在している場合は、副詞に強勢が移動する。

 He ˈput his hat ˈon.

 He ˈtook his shoes ˈoff.

(6) 以下の例のように、spontaneous speech では、しばしば副詞の強勢が抑制される。

 a. She ˈ*broke out* in ˈtears.

 b. I ˈ*woke up* in ˈhospital.

 c. The rain ˈ*went on* for ˈhours.

 d. He ˈ*came in* with a ˈteacup in his hand.

 e. Her face ˈ*brightened up* at the ˈthought.

 f. She ˈ*comes on* ˈstrong sometimes.　（言い方がきつい）

 g. Then he ˈ*came up* with an i ↘dea.　（ある考えを思いついた）

ここでも the rule of three が働いている。なお、3 つの強勢音節が隣り合わせにならずに無強勢音節が存在しているケースも多い。上記の例文はまさにその証しである。実は、the rule of three の適用には少し幅があって、強勢音節の間に余分の（複数の）無強勢の音節が存在する方がいっそう口調（語呂）がよい。ロンドンに Piccadilly Circus という観光名所がある。ˌPiccaˈdilly ˈCircus と言っても、-ly という無強勢音節があり、このままでも強勢の衝突（stress clash）が起らない。しかし、余分の弱勢がある方が語呂がいいので、強勢の位置を前に移動して、ˈPiccadilly ˈCircus と言うのが一般的である。

課題 20　　**Adverbs of place**（再訪）

　先ず、There is a book on the table. はどのようなイントネーションで発音されるか。どこに核強勢が来るか。その定番である末尾の table だろうか。実は、book が核強勢を受けるというのが中立的なパターンである。このような核強勢配置になるのはなぜだろうか。まず、the table に定冠詞がついているので、on the table は情報的に no real news ではないことは明白である。ここで「時間と場所の副詞」における強勢配置の規則を整理しておこう。

> Although adverbs in general are usually highlighted, adverbs and adverbial phrases of **time** and **place** are often not highlighted when at the end of an intonation group, even if they contain new information.

場所の表現がしばしば核強勢を受けない理由は、その場所が馴染みであるとか、身近にあるとか、文脈に存在することを聞き手に暗示するので、場所を明示しても、そこには特に目新しい情報がないと見做されるからである。

a. Waiter, I ˈfound a ↘fly *in my soup*.
b. He's ˈgot a tat ↘too *on his arm*.
c. There's ↘snow *in the wind*.
d. There's a ˈsign of ↘spring *in the air*.
e. Alan, there's a mos ↘quito *on your arm*!
f. You ˈlook like ˈFather ↘↗Christmas / with ˈall that ↘snow *on your coat*.
g. ˈHow did you ˈget that ↘oil *on your face*?

以下は、慣用表現について私と海外の研究者との公開ディスカッションの一部である。先ず、私の発信内容（SUPRAS, July 17, 2002）を紹介しよう。

　Dear all

　I understand from Bolinger (1986:121) that the following sentences with idiomatic expressions are supposed to have the nucleus occur earlier on the noun object rather than on the sentence-final noun:

　1) She has a good HEAD on her shoulders. (=She's clever.)
　2) Stop trying to pull the WOOL over my eyes. (=Stop trying to deceive me.)
　3) Sit down. Take the LOAD off your feet. (=Rest your feet.)
　4) She's got a BEE in her bonnet. (=She's crazy.)

　Is the position of nucleus placement obligatory? Is there any other option,

depending on the intention or attitude of the speaker?
私は、核強勢の位置は、話者の態度によって移動することはあり得るかどうかを尋ねた。以下は、公開返信の一部である。

> I've tossed Tami's question around with my colleagues here, both in ESL and linguistics. While it raised several eyebrows and caused others to tilt their heads in reflection, none of us could think of an occasion where it would be appropriate to move the stress. One comment: only if by saying *"You've got a good head on your SHOULders"*, you mean "as opposed to the one sitting on your LAP."

実際には、上記のような対比用法はナンセンスである。一方、以下は、対比用法である。

    He's ˈgot a tatˈtoo on *his* ↘ *arm*. （not on his leg）

    There's a ˈfly in *my* ↘ *soup*. （not in my salad）

しかし、時には、末尾の locative に情報的価値を認めて例外的に核強勢を置くこともある。「こともあろうにこんな所に」(here of all places) とか「よりによってあんな所に」(there of all places) というニュアンスがある。

    h. I ˈfound a ˈpiccolo in my ↘ mailbox. （⇒ a 'news' locative「意外な場所」）

    i. I ˈleft my ˈcar in a ˈtow-away ↘ zone.
                     （⇒違法駐車をしている車はレッカー車で撤去される区域）

課題 21　　The house is on the hill. vs. The house is on fire.

　標題の 2 文は、藪から棒の（out-of-the-blue）発言と考える。即ち、house は共に初出である。では、それぞれの文のイントネーションはどのようになるだろうか。特に、核強勢はどの語に来るだろうか。

　　　The ˈhouse is on the ↘hill.
　　　The ↘house is on fire.

となる。前者は恒常的状態の描写であり、後者は状態の変化 ── 緊急事態 ── に注意を喚起している。ここで言う状態の変化とは、a change from the previous state of <u>not</u> being on fire である。次のペアーも突発的発言のイントネーションはである。

　　　Your ˈeyes are ↘blue.
　　　Your ↘eyes are red.

やはり前者は恒常的状態の描写であり、後者は、目が充血し赤いことに警告を発している。聞き手は、既にそれに気づいているかもしれないが、話し手には関心事になっている。文献にある解説を見てみよう。

　　　They differ in that the redness of the pair of eyes would be taken to be of a temporary kind, but the blueness of the other pair is of a permanent type...

　　　　　　　　　　　　　　　　　Gussenhoven, *On Accent* (1983:20)

余談になるが、Gussenhoven は、Your ↘eyes are blue. の例を挙げている。聖書の創世記での或る場面を想定している。「なるほど」と思える。

　　　Adam (upon first seeing Eve): Your ↘eyes are blue!
　　　Eve: Pardon?
　　　Adam: Your eyes! They're blue! I love blue!

ここでは、状態の変化ではなく、関心の強さ故に、eyes が核強勢を受けている。
　次に、ルーブル美術館で、観光ガイドとツアーグループが、古代ギリシアの女神像の前で足を止める。像は頭部が欠けている。ガイドは、次のように言う。（ご覧のように）The ˈhead is ↘missing.
それは、既に established fact である。一方、休館日に美術館の警備員が巡回中に「大変だ。像の首がもぎ取られている！」と叫び声を上げるときは

　　　Oh, my God! The ↘head is missing!

また、ミルクの性質は動物性であるという恒常的性質のことを言っている場合、

¹Milk is ↘ animal.

一方、ミルクが、屋内や冷蔵庫から戸外に取り出され、日なたに放置されている異常事態に注意を喚起し、善処しなさいという場合、

The ↘ milk is in the sun.

ドアーが開いている状態も、語用論的解釈が関わってくる。

a. A: Hi, Jane.
B: Jack! How did you get in the building?
A: The ¹door's ↘↗ open.
B: Oh, I thought I locked it.

b. A: OK, everybody. Now get in the car. We're ready to go.
B: Uh-oh. Wait a second.
A: What's wrong?
B: The ↘ door's open.

Knowles にある解説を紹介しよう。

> The dynamic predicate rule is used strategically in conversation to indicate that an event or change of state is necessary, or that something is wrong: the *DOOR's open* may be interpreted not as a statement about the door, but as a command to shut it and *the WATER's too cold* is likely to be something more than a description of the water, e.g., it might indicate refusal to go swimming.
>
> *Patterns of Spoken English* (1987:151)

c. A: What's the matter?
B: The ↘ battery's dead.

d. A: Why's the teacher upset?
B: The ↘ floor's dirty.

e. A: Why are you taking the afternoon off?
B: My ↘ son's sick.

なお、今回のテーマは、課題 45 の event sentence と連動している。

課題 22   That's funny.

　英語には、<u>1つの文に核強勢が2つ存在する</u>という異例なパターンが存在する。その場合は、通例、下降調＋上昇調という idiomatic intonation になる。例えば、*New Horizon* 2（旧版）の CD では Oh, ↘<u>that's</u> ↗<u>cool</u>. が聞かれる。今回は、以下に示す単純な文構造に的を絞って考察してみよう。

　　↘<u>That's</u> a ↗<u>pity</u>.
　　↘<u>That's</u> a re↗<u>lief</u>.
　　↘<u>That's</u> the ↗<u>spirit</u>.
　　↘<u>That's</u> my ↗<u>boy</u>.
　　↘<u>That's</u> a good ↗<u>girl</u>.
　　↘<u>That's</u> ↗<u>interesting</u>.
　　↘<u>That's</u> ↗<u>strange</u>.
　　↘<u>That's</u> a ↗<u>shame</u>.
　　↘<u>That's</u> ↗<u>right</u>.
　　↘<u>That's</u> a sur↗<u>prise</u>.
　　↘<u>That</u> sounds ↗<u>good</u>.

このようなパターンは説明がむつかしい。そもそも既知情報は、通例、文強勢を受けない。例えば、代名詞（he, she, it など）は、文強勢を受けないという原則がある。上記の例文中の指示代名詞 that についても同じことが言えるはずである。しかし、that が示す内容は、場面から容易に推測できるにもかかわらず、原則に反して文強勢（核強勢）を受けている。しかし、that を it に置き換えると、上記のような下降＋上昇調のパターンにはならない。つまり、以下の3例はあり得ないパターンである。

　　* ↘<u>It's</u> ↗<u>funny</u>.
　　* ↘<u>It's</u> a ↗<u>pity</u>.
　　* ↘<u>It's</u> the ↗<u>spirit</u>.

そう言えば、it を that に置き換えると、that が核強勢を受けるのは定番であるように思える。典型的ケースは、What's <u>that</u> supposed to mean? である。これは、matter-of-fact ではなく、emotionally charged (colored) な発言で、相手の言ったことに「ムカッと」したときに発せられる。

　　a. A: Did you say you want to lose 30 pounds? But just words won't work.

  B: ¹*What's* ↘ *that supposed to mean*? Are you implying that I'll never make it?

  A: Action speaks louder than words, you know.

 b. A: My neck hurts.

  B: You should take up yoga.

  A: ¹*How will* ↘ *that help*?

 c. A: Your face is bruised.

  B: Yeah, I walked into the door.

  A: ¹*Where did* ↘ *that happen*?

 d. A: Didn't you hear the news? It was on TV. Carlos Ghosn was arrested. For phony business transactions.

  B: (in surprise) Well, ¹*how do you* ¹*like* ↘ *that*?　（こりゃ驚きだ）

 e. A: I was in Nepal. It's a small country just north of India.

  B:¹*What was* ↘ *that* like?

「賛同」を表す表現

 f. A: It'll be nice to have some time off.

  B: You can ¹*say* ↘ *that again*.

以下は、「もしそれが現実になったら、それは特別な日になる」という意味から、「まさか！」「そんなことあり得ない！」という実際に起こりそうにないと思っていることに使う表現である。

 g. A: I'm going to quit drinking.

  B: Really? ↘ *That'll be the* ↗ *day*.

  A: I'm really serious this time

 h. A: John says he'll start to work out at the gym.

  B: ↘ *That'll be the* ↗ *day.*

逆説的な意味をもつ表現がもう1つある。それは、I like that. である。「あきれた！」、「それはないよ！」という否定的な意味がある。

 i. ［待ち合わせの場所に誤解があった］

  A: I thought you were never coming.

  B: (Angrily) *I like* ↘ *that*! After keeping me waiting so long.

 j. A: You're making a fool of yourself.

課題 22　　That's funny.

　　　　B: I'm making a fool of myself? *I like ↘that*!
ちょっと興味深い記述がある。
　「留学生に英語を教えている D 先生が、どうも生徒の反応がかんばしくない。どこか理解に欠けるところがあるので、教科書をもう一度振り返ってみると、I like that. にその原因があることに気づいた。文脈では「私、そんなの嫌だわ」の意味になる個所だった。」
　　　　　　　　　　　　　松香洋子『娘と私の英語留学記』（1987:45）
しかし、下降調だけのパターンを時々聞くこともある
　　　ˈThat's the ↘spirit.
　　　ˈThat ⁽¹⁾sounds ↘great!
　　　ˈThat's no ⁽¹⁾way to ↘talk.
また、that が、文強勢を受けないケースもある。
　　　I ˈdidn't ↘know that.
　　　I ˈdon't ↘like that.
　　　I ˈhate ˈpeople who ↘lie like that.

課題 23　　　下降＋上昇調の返答文

先ず、2つの返答文の例を挙げよう。

  a.　A: Are you going?
     B₁: ↘ Yes, I ↘ am.
     B₂: ↘ Yes, I ↘ am going.

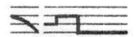

     Yés, I ám going.

B₁ と B₂ のイントネーションには誰も馴染みがあるだろう。しかし、もう1つ返答法もあり、それも、ネーティブスピーカーの間ではよく使われるイントネーション型 ── 下降調＋上昇調 ── である。

     ↗ Yes, ↘ I'm ↗ going.

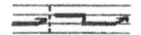

     Yés, I'm going.

ただし、この場合の下降・上昇調は、B₁ と B₂ のイントネーションと比べて、少しニューアンスに違いがある。それは、話者が、少なくとも自分には自明に（obvious）思える質問に対して、我慢強く、丁寧に ── with patience and courtesy ── 答えるときのイントネーションである（p.99 参照）。

私は、第1章「概論」の中で、「核強勢を受ける語は、新情報を伝える部分（領域）の最後の内容語である」と述べている。しかし、この返答文には、新情報の内容語はない。それにもかかわらず、全体として ↘ I'm ↗ going. というイントネーションになる。他者との対比でもないのに I に核強勢があると宣言するには論理的に無理がある。しかし going が末尾で上昇調になるのはそれが 'given' information であるからとも言えるし、または、「丁寧、相手を安心させる」とも解釈できる。

　概して言えば、「下降＋上昇調（通例、低上昇調）」のような複合音調のイントネーションは、日本人には全く馴染みのない型であるが、中学の検定教科書の音声資料を聞いていると、時々、聞かれる。例えば、

  b.　A: Do you know him?
     B: ↗ Yes, ↘ I know ↗ him.

課題 23　　下降＋上昇調の返答文

 c. Mother: Don't forget to do your home work.

   Daughter: I've already done that.

   Mother: That's great! Oh, will you pick up your little brother?
     He's at Aunt Peg's house.

Daughter: Sure, ↘I'll pick him ↗up.

この対話を Wells に紹介した。以下の教示を受けた。

 On balance, I think the most likely pattern for these utterances is fall plus rise...The problem is that the answers contain no new material or grammatical items. So there is no non-'given' item to place the nucleus. I have to say, though, that I don't feel very pleased with my explanation so far. Or perhaps we can just say they're yet more intonational idioms.

もう少し例を挙げておこう。

 a. A: Where you from?

   B: I'm originally from Sydney, Australia. But I live in Paris now.

   A: Do you speak French?

   B: ↘Yes, ↘I speak ↗French.

 b. A: Where were you born?

   B: In Rio de Janeiro.

   A: Are you Brazilian?

   B: ↘Yes, ↘I'm Bra↗zilian.

 c. A: Do you see the girl with short hair near the table?

   B: ↗Yes, ↘I see ↗her. Who is she?

EP Book One にも幾つか例がある。

 d. A: Do you see two seats and the bookshelves between the windows?
    Do you see the clock over the bookshelves?

   B: Yes, I ↘see ↗them. (p.47)

 e. Where are you, Mary?

   ↘Here is ↗Mary. She is coming into the room. She says, " ↘Here I ↗am." (p.69)

課題 24　　前置詞に置かれる不可解な文強勢

先日、リスニング教材の CD を聴いていると、「おや！」と思う発音があった。まず、教材を示そう。

A: Excuse me. I think I'm lost. Is there a movie theater near here?
B: Let me see. Oh, yes. There's one on Spring Street.
A: ˈWhere ↘on Spring Street?
B: It's on the corner of Spring Street and Park Avenue. You can't miss it. It's across from the post office.
A: Thank you!

論理的には、↘Where on Spring Street? であるべきである。なぜ、where をさしおいて、機能語 on ── しかも、反復語である ── が文強勢（ここでは核強勢）を受けて言われたのか。話者の意図は、いったい何だろうか。この on は他の前置詞と対比されているのではない。学習者には、全く不可解な強勢配置である。
一方、以下の対話では、on が文強勢（核強勢）を受けるのは理に叶っている。

A: Excuse me. Where is the restaurant in this hotel?
B: Ah. Take the lift to the first floor.
A: I'm sorry. I don't understand.
B: The restaurant. It's on the first floor. So, take the lift...
A: You mean 'elevator'.
B: Yes. Yes, of course. Take the elevator to the first floor.
A: But we're ↘on the first floor now.
B: No, no. This is the ground floor.
A: Aha! You're British.

実は、論理的理由もなく、前置詞を強調して発音するのは、英語母語話者に時折見られる珍現象である。英語の音声学では、時折、話題になる。Wells の phonetic blog には

Girl: Daddy, I want to sit on the window side.
Boy: But you're ↘on the window side.

標準的な言い方は、

But you ↘are on the window side. または
But you're ↘sitting on the window side. である。　　(February 21, 2008)

課題 24　　前置詞に置かれる不可解な文強勢

更にもう 1 例を紹介しよう。
　A: Well, why don't you take a little time off? I want you at your best.
　B: I'm ↘ at my best. I won't let you down.
標準的な言い方は
　I ↘ am at my best. である。

さて、Where on Spring Street? の例に接して、海外の研究者の反応を知るために、私は、SUPRAS に次のようなメールを一斉発信した。

> Would it be possible for native speakers to utter the underlined part with the nucleus on the preposition in some pragmatic context? I think I heard a voice actor do so. I presume that normally they would emphasize the interrogative.

いろいろな返信があった。

(1) Hi, Tami. Like you, I would stress the 'Where' (as a native speaker). But I think it is becoming increasingly possible for even native speakers to stress the preposition. Evolution, I guess. Mustn't grumble. Sue

(2) I agree with Sue. Strange but true. I'll try and listen out for other comparable examples.

(3) I just caught the following two tone units on BBC radio:
| WITH the queen | AT Buckingham Palace ...

(4) It is a constructed dialogue with an actor speaking; and so the actor could be faulted in the way that the other colleagues have suggested – that the tonic should accompany "Where". This kind of thing sometimes happens in news reading from a script.

(5) It's what happens when people go into automatic mode.

ニュースを聞いていると、レポーターが、対比や強調でもないのに前置詞に文強勢を置いていることがしばしばある。

"A report | ON today's proceedings | IN the parliament will be given | BY John Smith..."

機内アナウンスでも、時々、このようなアブノーマルな発音を耳にすることがある。例えば、in-flight safety announcements である。離陸前、attendant がマニュアル（fixed script）を朗読するときに起こることがある。

(i) "Good morning. ladies and gentlemen. Welcome aboard Korean Air flight 493 bound | FOR Taipei. We are sorry | FOR the delay |IN our departure....."

(ii) "IN the event | OF an emergency | there will be emergency lighting | IN the aisles |

ほかに、対比目的以外で前置詞を強調する傾向は、以下のような短い慣用表現にも頻繁に聞かれる。

a. (i) There! I ↘beat you to it.　（どうだ君を負かしただろう）

　(ii) There! I ˈbeat you ↘to it.

b. A:（ゴルフの誘い）Next Sunday. No excuses!

　B: All right.

　A(i): I'll ↘hold you to it.　（約束は守れよ）

　A(ii): I'll ˈhold you ↘to it.

c. (i) ↘Stick to it.　（最後まで頑張れ！）

　(ii) ˈStick ↘to it.

d. (i) ↘Get to it.　（かかれ）

　(ii) ˈGet ↘to it.

e. (i) ↘Here's to you. Your very good health!

　(ii) ˈHere's ↘to you.

映画『ローマの休日』の中で、新聞記者 Joe(A) が王女 Ann(B) に初めての喫煙の感想を聞く。

A: Your first cigarette, hm? Well, what's the verdict?

B: ˈNothing ↘to it.

A: That's right ― ˈnothing ↘to it.

映画『ある夜の出来事』で

A: Peter! Peter!

B: What's the matter?

A: I was so scared.

B: ˈWhat's got ↘into you? I was gone only a minute.

『ある貴婦人の肖像』では、甲斐性のない Osmond（娘の交際相手）について、

Mother: There is nothing ↘of him: no money, no name, no importance.
　　　　Don't you care for these things?

課題 24　　前置詞に置かれる不可解な文強勢

かつて Jack Windsor Lewis に、このような不可解な強勢について教示を求めたことがある。

    No easy explanation occurs to me immediately re
    There's nothing \of him.

Lots of prepositions behave this way, e.g.:

    There's nothing \to it
    There's nothing \in it
    There's nothing \for it
    I'm looking \at it
    I get nothing \from it
    Far \from it
    No doubt a\bout it
    Get \with it
    Think nothing \of it

For now I haven't the time to try to say anything more helpful, but I hope to look again at some of your puzzles at some time.　　(September 21, 2006)

課題 25　　文頭における高いピッチ：その問題点

　日本人の英語発音の特徴の一つとして、文頭を高いピッチで始めるというのは、よく知られている。それ故に、日本人の英語は「尻下り」だと言われることがある。私が、このことを SUPRAS 上で言及すると、R. Dauer（*Accurate English* の著者、故人）から以下の返信があった。

> I fully appreciate the need you have expressed to teach intonation to Japanese students. I find I must always explain that they must not begin in a sentence with "I" (or any other pronoun) on a high pitch, as it may be misinterpreted by a native speaker as meaning "I'm better than you" or "I do this, but you don't." (2002.12.21)

確かに、多くの日本人は、英語で自己紹介をするとき、⁻My name is... とか、⁻I like ... というように、冒頭の語を高く言う傾向がある。しかし、ネーティブスピーカーも、時折、そのように言うことがあるので、日本人の癖を間違っているとは言えないこともある。問題は、その頻度である。英語では、音調単位の冒頭にある無強勢音節 ── しばしば代名詞と冠詞 ── が、通常よりも高いピッチで言われることがある。high prehead（高前頭部）と呼ばれる。それにより、発言全体が lively, interested になる効果がある。

a.　⁻I'm ˈsimply ↘<u>fam</u>ished.
b.　[Do you like wine?] ⁻I ↘<u>love</u> it.
c.　[I just have bread and coke for breakfast.] ⁻You're ↘<u>crazy</u>.
d.　⁻I saw you with ↘<u>Jane</u> last night.

また、high onset もある。例えば、

e.　A: I'm going to the wedding.
　　B: ⁻Who's getting ↘<u>married</u>?

e の場合、who は高いピッチで始まり目立って発音されているが、このパターンは高い関心のシグナルとなる。

> Suppose someone you know well tells you that he or she is going to a wedding. Depending on how much <u>interest</u> this fact arouses in you, you might say *Who's getting married?* either with a low (or non-high) onset or with a high onset.
> 　　　　　　　　　　Kreidler, *Describing Spoken English* (1997)

課題 25　文頭における高いピッチ：その問題点

また、*New Horizon* 2 には、ホームステイしている生徒が、ある悩みを先生に告げている箇所がある。先生は以下のように助言する。

>　You must tell your host mother. Say, "I'm sorry. The food tastes delicious, but I can't eat that much. ⁻She'll under ↗ stand."

CD を聴くと、she が高くなっている。なお、末尾で上昇調になっているのは、encouraging や reassuring のシグナルである。

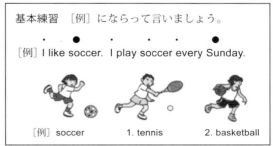

　5，6 年前、いろいろな中学校教科書の準拠音声を点検していた。*New Horizon* 1、Unit 3 を見て私は驚いた。絵にあるように I に強勢マークが付記されてある。最初の I like soccer. は、ひどい！　これは high prehead を文強勢と誤解している。そのように誤解すると、文強勢が 3 連続することになり、「3 連規則」により、中間にある like の強勢が抑制されると解釈しているように思える。教師と生徒たちは、なぜ重要な動詞 like が「強く、はっきりと」発音されていないのかと戸惑ったに違いない。しかも、指導書（teacher's guide）には、何の解説もない。更に嘆かわしいのは、生徒は、それ以後は I に強勢を置く癖を身に付けるだろう。図中の文を high prehead で読むこと自体には問題はないが、強勢表記法に問題がある。いや、それよりも音声収録方針に問題がある。入門期の英語学習であることを考慮し、責任者が収録に立ち会い、voice actor たちに標準的な読み方をするよう指示するべきであった。私は、啓林館の *Listening Box* シリーズを他の 2 名と分担して執筆した経験がある。音声収録にも立ち会った。ガラス越しに録音室の voice actor を聴き、教育的観点から具合が悪い発音がすると合図を送り、録音ブースに入って修正をお願いした。余談だが、出版社が契約しているプロの声優は掛け持ちの収録の仕事をしており、新年度前の数カ月はとても忙しい。原稿を初見しただけで本番に入る。だから、時間制で報酬を支払う出版社から重宝される。私が立ち合ったときも、リハーサルはなしだった。中高のリスニング教材なので、数分間、原稿に目を通すだけであった。声優に任せきりにすると、ネーティブスピーカーの感覚からみて、自然で colloquial な読み方をする。残念なことに、それは、入門期の graded steps を踏まえた、いわば楷書式の発音ではないこと

もある。

　New Horizon 1 に戻ると、確かに準拠 CD で聞く英語のほうが生き生きして臨場感を与えるだろうが、英語を EFL として学習する段階を無視してはいけない。いの一番に I ˈlike ↘ soccer. を導入するべきだった。˥I like ↘ soccer. は、too advanced である。

　参考までに、Jack Windsor Lewis に音声資料を送りコメント求めた。以下は、その一部である。

> I was interested to listen to the extracts. You're right that the 'I's with their repeated high falls sound accented and at the same time animated. However, in the cases we have they sound quite natural — if rather a little over-enthusiastic for the taste of some people.

確かに、Lewis は音声資料の質をいちおう評価している。問題なのは、入門期の生徒に対する教育的配慮である。いくら自然な音声とはいっても、EFL 教科書の Lesson 1 に教えるべきではない。後遺症が残り、百害あって一利なしである。

課題 26　　　賛同、激励、賞賛を表す決まり文句

Baby Blues という 30 年もの長きにわたってアメリカで連載されている漫画がある。ある若い夫婦による 3 人の子どもの躾け・教育の苦労を滑稽に描いている。英語音声学を研究している者には baby talk の発音は興味深い。今回は、それと絡めて、ユニークな idiomatic intonation を紹介しよう。激励や賞賛を表す決まり文句である。

Mother: [looking out of the window] Zoe! Grandma and Grandpa are here.
Zoe: Yay! Gwandma! Gwandpa!
Grandma: There's my girl!
Grandpa: Hi, sweetheart!
Mother: Pop, I told you not to bring her any candy.
Grandpa: I know, but I thought one piece would be okay.
Zoe: I wike him!
Father: Let's have a drink.
Grandpa: Now there's a thought.

さて、baby talk には以下の特徴がある。

(i) /l/ と /r/ → [w] : like → *wike*, little → *widdle*, crazy → *cwazy*, grand → *gwand*

(ii) /θ/ → [f]: three → *fwee*

(iii) /ð/ → [d]: these → *dese*, that → *dat*

一般に、幼児が子音を習得するには段階があって、まず、口の前付近で作る音（m, n, p, b, t, d, w）は、最も易しいので早く修得（acquired）される。一番早く修得される唇を使う音 papa と mama は、その典型例である。また、/w/ も唇を使う音である。一方、調音に際して、もっと「複雑な」操作を必要とする音（l, r, s, th）は難しく 5 歳ぐらいまでかかる。

> Many children learning English as an L1 will have mastered the vowel system by the age of three, but many will take at least until the age of five to master the system of consonants. Thus, little special guidance is usually necessary for learning vowels, but often particular guidance will help children to master the consonants.
>
> Cruttenden, *Gimson's Pronunciation of English* (2014: 6)

さて、上記の下線部のイントネーションを考えてみよう。私が「概論」で述べた規則に従えば、核強勢は girl と thought に来るはずである。

  There's my ↘girl.

 'Now there's a ↘thought.

しかし、人を激励、賞賛、慰めを表す短い成句は、多くの場合、複合音調「下降＋（低）上昇調」で言われる。

  ↘There's my ↗girl.

  ↘There's a ↗thought.

私の友人のアメリカ人大学教授は、次のように言う。

  It's hard to express, but it seems to me that the rises on 'girl' and 'thought' indicate a friendly, inviting attitude.

イギリス人 Wells も次のように言う。

  These typically have a Fall plus Rise.

   \That's a good /girl.

   \That's the /spirit.

   \That's no way to /talk.

  Though they can also be said with an early High Fall:

   \That's a good girl.

   \That's the spirit.

   \That's no way to talk.

a. A: I painted it myself, Daddy.

  B: ↘There's a clever ↗boy.

b. A: I've been helping Mummy, Daddy.

  B: ↘That's a good ↗girl.

店で写真にあるような犬を見かけたら

c. ↘There's a clever ↗dog.

誰かから妙案を聞いて

d. ↘There's an i↗dea.

なお、that が there に取って代わることがある。

  ↘That's my ↗boy(girl).

  ↘That's a ↗thought.

  ↘That's the ↗spirit.

課題 26　賛同、激励、賞賛を表す決まり文句

　また、That's [There's] my boy (girl). に代わって、That's the boy と That's the girl. という激励や賞賛の表現もある。やはり、前者と同じイントネーションで発せられる。更には、もっとくだけた表現 Attaboy! と Attagirl! もある。核強勢は最初の音節に来る。

　A: Daddy, I won the spelling bee.　（スペリング・コンテスト）
　B: ↘Attaboy!
　　　↘Attagirl!

課題 27   Obvious questions

Free Willy は、20世紀末に一世を風靡したアメリカ映画である。第2部と第3部も制作された。母親に捨てられた少年 Jessie と、無理やり家族から引き離されたシャチの Willy との絆を中心に、互いに孤独な境遇の中で交流を深め、成長していく姿を美しい自然の中で描いた映画であった。Jessie と飼育係 Rae は、Willy に芸を教えることに情熱を注ぐ。ある日、Willy の芸を観客に披露すると大受けした。ショーの後、少年（A）は水族館の責任者（B）から呼ばれる。以下は、その時の会話である。

 A: Did you see him?
 B: Yes, I did. You can do all that again? What you and Rae want costs money. I must be sure.
 A: <u>Dogs pee on brick walls?</u> I mean, yes, sir. We can do it again.

私は、当時、ビデオで何度も聞き直したが、全くチンプンカンプンであった。上昇調の発言であったので yes-no 疑問文らしいと推測したが、それにしても、後の I mean, yes, sir と意味的に繋がらない。*Free Willy* の screen play を見て、ようやく意味が分かった。少年は、次のように言っていた。

 ↘Dogs | ˈpee on ˈbrick ↗ walls?
  参考：2つの音調単位に分かれる。Dogs は新情報の名詞であるので、major information として独自の音調単位になる。

犬が壁に小便するのは習性であり、当たり前のことである。従って、Yes, of course. という意味である。このような独特の obvious question が他にも存在する。例えば、

 A: Are you hungry?
 B: Does a bear shit in the woods?　　（クマって森でウンコする？）

以下も逆質問として使える。

 Do fish swim?
 Is the sky blue?

しかし、最もオーソドックスな obvious question ── 逆質問 ── を、私は実体験した。ある日、予想外に長引く教授会にうんざりし、横にいる年配のアメリ

課題 27　Obvious questions

カ人教員に、「少し休憩したくない？」という意味のことを言ったら、彼は真顔で "Is the Pope Catholic?" と呟いた。ローマ教皇がカトリックであるのは当たり前のこと。

　　A: Would you like to go to the beach?
　　B: Is the Pope Catholic?

以上のような obvious question を聞かれたら、クソ真面目に Yes, he is. と言ってはいけない。聞き流すだけでいい。しかし、人びとは、時には、社交上で obvious とは言えなくても、さりげない、とりとめのない質問を発することもある。そんな時は、相手の人は上昇調で応える。その理由は、以下で述べられている。

　　Often answers with this (rising) intonation are given to questions that may seem pointless or silly. The rising intonation indicates that the answerer has decided to treat the question with courtesy and patience and to assume the questioner had a legitimate reason for asking it.

　　English Language Services, INC, *Stress and Intonation* Part 2 (p.48)

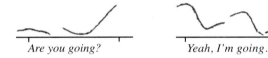
　　　Are you going?　　　　Yeah, I'm going.

a.　A: Are you going?
　　B: Yeah, ↘ I'm ↗ going.
b.　A: Is this a book?
　　B: Yes. ↘ It's a ↗ book.
c.　A: Is this a chair?
　　B: Yes. ↘ It's a ↗ chair.
d.　A: What's that in your hand? Is it a camera?
　　B: Yes, ↘ this is a ↗ camera.

なお、Yes, I'm going. や Yes, it's a book. 等のイントネーションの表記法について、本項では、── 便宜的に ── 代名詞が文強勢（核強勢）を受けるとしているが、むしろ high prehead（p.92 参照）の発音であるという見方もあろう。これは、聴覚的には両者の区別ができない 1 例である。また、Yes, this is a camera. でも、this は核強勢を受けるのか、または、単に high onset（同ページ参照）であるかの聞き分けが難しい。本項では、前者を採用している。

課題 28　　double words の強勢

英語では、double words が「本物の」(genuine) の意味を表すときに使われる。これらの表現は、複合語 (compound) であるので、最初の語が強勢を受ける。以下のようなコンテクストで使われる。

a. I don't particularly like instant coffee. Do you ˈhave ↗ coffee coffee?
b. A: Do you wear a hat?
   B: Well, I ˈdon't really wear a ↘ hat hat; just something to keep the sun off.

念のために、私の同僚のアメリカ人に確認した。

"Coffee coffee" is an expression that means real coffee, not instant, not decaffeinated and not flavored. I don't use the expression, but I immediately understand it. I can only think of one other similar expression, **beer beer** (a real beer, not a low-calorie beer, non-alcohol beer or in Japan *happoshu* beer).

また、カナダ人の同僚にも確認すると、

Yes, we do use double words like this to mean authentic things or people. I actually do like **beer beer**, not that American watered-down stuff. Also, my friend is a **pilot pilot**, not like my brother who can only fly single-propeller planes. It is used very casually, and usually to make people laugh.

John Wells からもコメントがあった。

It has compound stress. "Give me some BEER beer." Of course, contrastive stressing would lead to the same result: Not NEAR beer, but BEER beer.

c. A: Is she Korean?
   B: Yeah.
   A: Korean-Korean, or Korean-American?
   B: Oh, she's Korean-Korean, but she went to high school in Vermont.
d. Is she Italian-Italian or Italian-American?
e. Is this a Chevy-Chevy or an Isuzu?

日本語には、同じ語を繰り返して意味を強める double words が多い。雪がしんしんと降る、びしびし鍛える、こつこつ努力するなど。インドやシンガポー

課題 28　　double words の強勢

ルなど東南アジアの英語では形容詞の double words がよく聞かれる。例えば、cheap cheap, hot hot, good good などがある。かつて、イギリスの女子フットボールを題材にした映画『ベッカムに恋して』（*Bend it Like Beckham*）を見ていたとき、苦笑したことがある。インド系の女子高校生がユニフォームに着替えている場に居合わせたインド人の叔母が、姪の若い breasts を見て juicy juicy mangos と言っていた。何と訳せばいいのだろう。

　英語では擬音語に double words, triple words が豊富に存在する。

馬の蹄の音 clop! clippity, clop, clippity
ドスン、ドスン bump, bumpity, bump
水のしたたり drip, drippity, drip
ダンスのタップ tap, tappity, tap
タイプライターの音 clack, clackity, clack
お喋りのペチャクチャ blah, blah, blah / yak, yakety, yak
機関車のしゅぽ、しゅぽ toot-toot / choo-choo
柱時計 tick tock, tick tock

　要するに、形容詞の double words ― cheap cheap, juicy juicy ―が a higher degree を伝えるのに対して、名詞の double words ― beer beer, coffee coffee ―は、<u>genuine</u> version を暗示している。なお、<u>various</u> degrees（「様々な」）を暗示する場合、同じ語を等位接続詞 and で繋ぎ、「ピンからキリまで」の意味を伝える。

　　There are ˈteachers and ↘teachers.
　　There are ˈdictionaries and ↘dictionaries.
　　I like city life, but there are ˈcities and ↘cities.

課題 29　　What is that? の 3 種のイントネーション

EP Book One (p.65) には、以下の内容がある。

John's hat! と、感嘆詞があるのは、驚きや予想外の発見を示唆しているのであろう。右図中の 2 つ目の What is that? は、最初のものとは意味が違い、それ故に、イントネーションも違う。前者は information を求めている WH 疑問文であり、中立的なイントネーションでは下降調になるか、または、more friendly, more polite な態度を表す場合には、上昇調になる。どちらになるかは optional である。

ˈWhat is ↘that?　or　ˈWhat is ↗that?

一方、What is that? John's hat. は、情報を求めるのではなく、確認しながらも驚いていることを表している。この場合、<u>イントネーションは、必ず上昇になる</u>。それならば、上記の上昇調 ˈWhat is ↗that? と同じではないか、と思うかも知れないが、実際には、両者には大きな違いがある。前者では、上昇調は、核強勢のある that を起点として起こるが、後者では、核強勢は what にあり、上昇調は文の冒頭から始まる。

↗<u>What is that?</u>

聞くに際して注意しないといけないのは、いずれのケースでも that が上昇調のイントネーションの末尾にあり、声（pitch）が最も高くて目立って聞こえるので、後者でも、that があたかも核強勢を受けるように感じるかも知れない。後者の場合、what をしっかりと上昇調で言い、that は上昇調を、いわば、締めくくるつもりで ── 余韻のつもりで ── 言えばよい。

蛇足になるが、ˈWhat is your ↘name? ˈWhat is your ↗name? ↗<u>What</u> is your name? という 3 種類のイントネーションが考えられるが、最後のものは、相

課題 29　　What is that? の 3 種のイントネーション

Patterns for question-word questions.
Normal:　　ˈWhat is your ↘ name?
Interested:　　ˈWhat is your ↗ name?
Repeated:　　↗ What is your name?

手の名前が聞き取れずに、「もう一度言ってください」という意味の pardon question である。また、What did you say your name was? という問い返しでも、核強勢は what に来る。

What did you say your name was?

末尾の was は、声が最も高いので目立って聞こえるが、肝心なことは、上昇調の起点が冒頭の what にあることである。EP Book One (p.74) には、同タイプのイントネーションが用いられる例がもう 1 か所ある。

She put the hat in the other room.
John went there and got it.

Who got it? John did.

この場合、↗ Who got it? は、驚きの表明ではなく、checking question と呼ばれるタイプで、確認する／念押しする働きがある。John went there and got it. という歴然とした事実があるにもかかわらず、情報を求める、下降調の ˈWho ↘ got it? というのは、ナンセンスである。
　私の持っている 3 種類の音声資料（Harvard 大学の Richards 編集による LP レコード、洋販版 CD、IBC 版 CD）を聞き比べてみた。p. 65 の 2 つ目の What is that? と p.74 の Who got it? を *sen-sit* を踏まえて発音しているのは LP 版だけで、CD 版は、両方とも、いわゆる、機械的棒読み（専門的には citation form）であり、授業中の使用には不適切である。確認のために、いろいろな checking question（pardon question）の模式図を示そう。疑問詞 what を起点として、声の調子が上向きになっている。

教室の音声学

注：課題1などで、疑問詞は、文強勢を受ける資格があるが、文（音調単位）の冒頭では核強勢を受けないと言ってきたが、上昇調の checking question （pardon question）は例外である。

課題 30　　既知情報を伝える低上昇調

ある中学検定教科書（旧版）*New Crown* I と *New Horizon* I (CD) には、次のようなイントネーションがある。

(i) 　A: Are you thirsty?
　　　B: No. I'm ↘ not ↗ thirsty.

(ii)　 A: Are you hungry?
　　　B: Yes, ↘ I'm ↗ hungry.

(iii)　A: Do you know her?
　　　B: Of ˈcourse, ↘ I know ↗ her.

教職課程で英語音声学を学んでいない教師は、このようなイントネーションをどのように理解しているのだろうか。EP に準拠した音声資料でも、教師が当惑するだろうと思われるイントネーションがある。特に、上昇調が yes/no 疑問文に用いられる音調と思い込んでいる場合、それを肯定文中で聞いたら、きっと「なんで？」と思うだろう。実は、肯定文での上昇調が Book 1 & 2 の音声資料で時折聞かれる。例えば、下記に示す

　　　No, it is not a hat.
　　　Here is the collar.

ここでは末尾が（低）上昇調になっている。文中では、hat は既知情報であるので、通常ならば、強勢を受けないで ↘ No, it is ↘ not a hat. となるはずだが、音声資料では ↘ No, it is ↘ not a ↗ hat. となっている。また、↘ Here's the collar. という代わりに、↘ Here's the ↗ collar. となっている。実際は、どちらでもいいのであるが、話者の態度に微妙なニュアンスの違いがある。このような文脈における intonational meaning を知っておくと、応用力が身に付くだろう。

"Is this a hat?"
"No, it is not a hat. It is a hand".
That is an answer.

"Has your coat a collar?"

"Yes, it has. Here is the collar".

This is a room.
What do you see in the room?
Do you see the floor and three walls of the room?
Do you see them?

Do you see a door and two windows?
Is one of the windows open?
Is the other window shut?
Do you see two seats and the bookshelves between them?
Do you see the clock over the bookshelves?
Yes, I see them.
These things are in the room. The room is in a house.

文脈で分かりきった語は、強勢を受けずに低い key で言うのが neutral intonation であるが、話者が、その語にもう少し重要度を付加したい（give some degree of importance）と感じるときは、それを低上昇調で言う。もし下降調にすると、その語を新情報扱いにするか、何か特別の理由があって強調することになるので具合いが悪い。前ページの右の例文中の Yes, I see them. についても 2 通りのイントネーションがある。

　　　↘ Yes, I ↘ see them.　　または

　　　↘ Yes, I ↘ see ↗ them.

応用例として

　　a.　A: Is that Mr. Jones?

　　　　B₁: ↘ Yes, ↘ that's him.　　（やや事務的）

　　　　B₂: ↘ Yes, ↘ that's ↗ him.

　　b.　A: Excuse me, but I'm here to see Mr. Date.

　　　　B₁: ↘ I'm Mr. Date.　　（やや事務的）

　　　　B₂: ↘ I'm Mr. ↗ Date.　　（より丁寧、愛想がよい）

　　c.　A: I've got some chocolate here.

　　　　B₁: Oh, ↘ good. I ↘ like chocolate.

　　　　B₂: Oh, ↘ good. I ↘ like ↗ chocolate.

c の場合、B₂ のパターンになるには 2 つの理由が考えられる。第 1 に、話者は反復語 chocolate の重要性を完全になくさずに、多少は重要視したいのである（give some degree of importance）。第 2 に、低上昇調を用いることにより、話し手は聞き手に会話を続けようというシグナルを送ることができる。このように、低上昇調は、主要な概念（通常、新情報の内容語）に続く、それほど重要ではないが完全には無視することができない概念を示す。更に言えば、低上昇調は、聞き手への懇願（appeal to the listener）をもたらし、chocolate について、話し続けようと（Come on—let's talk about it.）聞き手に勧めている。

　　d.　A: John Cleese is a very funny actor.

　　　　B: Oh, yes. I've ↘ seen ↗ him.

課題 30　　既知情報を伝える低上昇調

　　　　I've　↘ seen　↗ him.

　　　　―　　＼　　ノ　　　　(Come on—let's talk about him).

Roach, *English Phonetics and Phonology* (2000:177)

e. A: Are you angry?
   B: No, I'm ↘ not ↗ angry.
f. A: Please give me some water.
   B: ↘ Here's some ↗ water.
g. A: John's just arrived. He's 10 minutes late.
   B: I ↘ thought he'd be ↗ late.
h. A: We must go.
   B: I'm ↘ sorry you ˈcan't stay ↗ longer.
i. A (customer): Do you sell garden tools, please?
   B (shopkeeper): I'm afˈraid we ˈcan't ↘ help you, sir.
   A: Any idea where I should try?
   B: What about Cook's in the Market Place?
   A: That's an idea. I'll go down there now. Many thanks.
   B: Well, I'm ↘ sorry we ˈcan't ↗ help you.

Thompson, *Intonation Practice* (1981:11-12)

j. A: What's that vegetable called? It's long, thin, green, like a pencil. What's the word?
   B: Asparagus?
   A: Yeah, ↘ that's ↗ it.

課題 31　　冠詞の強勢

　ある春、京都での GDM セミナーで、模擬授業のデモを見ていたとき、つくづく感じたことがあった。それは、定冠詞と不定冠詞の使い分けの難しさである。先生が、手にもった風船を提示すると、「生徒たち」が一斉に指差しして ˈThat is the balˋloon. ˈThat is ˈin your ˋhand. と口々に言い始めた。私は、「おやっ？」と思った。風船は、目前

にあるとは言え、談話的には、まだ共通の話題（common ground）にもなっていないのだから、いきなり、**the** baloon と言うのは、唐突であり、困惑する。多分、「生徒たち」は、風船が目の前にあるから、それが既に場面に存在していると勘違いしたのだろう。あの場合は、ˈThat is a balˋloon. と言うべきであった。実際、そう言っている「生徒たち」もいた。This is a pen. と This is the pen. との違いを考えればいい。初めて pen を正式に聞き手の意識の中に導入する ── 話題に上げる ── ときは ˈThis is a ˋpen. となる。一方、This is the pen. は、This is the pen that I was talking about. である。先ほどの That is the balloon. も、That is the balloon I was talking about. (I heard about, etc.) という意味なので、「不適切発言」である。

　ただし、初出の名詞が the を伴って発せられる文がある。この場合、その名詞は話し手と聞き手の間で暗黙の了承事項になっているけれども、正式には、共通の話題にはなっていないので初出の扱いになる。以下は、学習者には、思いつかない the の用法だろう。暗黙の了承事項である。

　a.　A: Did you enjoy your trip to Vancouver?

　　　B: Yeah. It was fantastic. **The** ˈ*people* are so ˋnice.

　b.　A: How was your trip to Thailand?

　　　B: I had a wonderful time. **The** ˈ*food* was ˋgreat.

　さて、本論の冠詞の強勢発音の話題に入ろう。冠詞 the と a は、本来、機能語であるので無強勢であるが、例外的に強勢を受けることがある。その時、発音はそれぞれ /ðiː/ と /eɪ/ となる。では、どのような状況で、冠詞が強勢を受けるのだろうか。1 つ目は強調、そして、2 つ目は対比のためである。

課題 31　　冠詞の強勢

強調の用法：

a. ˈGDˈM is ˈ**the**/ðiː/ ⁽ˡ⁾ way to ˈteach ↘English.

　　(= GDM is the best method of teaching English.)

b. ˈ*English Through* ˈ*Pictures* is ˈ**the**/ðiː/ ⁽ˡ⁾book for ˈteaching ↘English.

c. Ah, ˈthis is ˈ**the**/ðiː/ ↘life!　　（人生、こうでなくちゃ！）

d. The ˈTokyo ⁽ˡ⁾Disney ˈSea is ˈ**the**/ðiː/ ⁽ˡ⁾place to ↘be now.

e. ˈIce-cold ˈbeer is ˈ**the**/ðiː/ ⁽ˡ⁾drink for a ˈhot ↘day like this.

対比の用法：

後続の名詞は既知情報であるので文強勢を受けない。冠詞が文強勢（しばしば核強勢）を受ける。

a. A: Is that the best way to do it?
   B: Well, it's ↘**a** /eɪ/ way to do it. But I'm not sure it's the best way.

b. A: Isn't Mrs. Jones a teacher at Bellview School?
   B: Yes. She is ↘**a** /eɪ/teacher. But she isn't my teacher.

c. A: Do you know Ms. Jones?
   B: Well, I know ↘**a** /eɪ/ Ms. Jones. But I don't know whether it's the same one.

d. A: What do you think of Bill's point of view?
   B: Well, it's ↘**a** /eɪ/ point of view. But it's not mine.

なお、私の友人（アメリカ人大学教授）は、次のようにコメントする。

　　Ok, but I personally would probably say/ʌ/ with sterss for emphasis.

蛇足になるが、the air, the eye のような場合、the は /ðɪ/ と発音しなければならないと教えられているが、実際には、/ðə/ のままでいい。洋販出版から出ている Ladder Edition シリーズ中の *The Wizard of Oz* と *The Adventures of Tom Sawyer* の朗読テープでは、母音直前の the は子音前と同じである。例えば、

・Gradually the balloon filled and rose into <u>the</u> air.

・Soon the Winged Monkey flew in through <u>the</u> open window.

・<u>The</u> other boys watched Tom.

・<u>The</u> hours passed.

このような発音は、既に Peter Ladefoged による音声学入門書 *A Course in Phonetics*（1993）にも記述がある。

> There is a growing tendency for younger American English speakers to use [this] form in all circumstances, even before a vowel.

私は、この傾向がティーン・エイジャーや 20 歳代の若者に限って使われる「若者ことば」なのかどうかを確かめるために海外の研究仲間にメールを発信した。すると、コロラドで ESL（English as a Second Language）を教えている女性から以下のような返信があった。

> I don't think it's only younger speakers who use the schwa/ə/ before vowels with the definite article. I do it all the time (44 years old) -- almost 100 % of the time. I tend to speak a little fast, perhaps. I think people do it in what we'd call fast speech, but the speech isn't always so fast, really. Perhaps it's a matter of simplification? I teach it to ESL students as a perfectly acceptable alternative that many native speakers use. I think, in general, that ESL teachers should be accepting of forms that native speakers use widely and welcome them in their ESL classes!

彼女も言うように、母音の前の the/ðə/ は fast speech だけに表れるのではない。先ほど挙げたストーリーの朗読は slower and more careful なものである。また、このような傾向はイギリス英語にも見られる。John Wells は *Longman Pronunciation Dictionary* の中でそのことを述べている。

また、今年（2019）春に出た Geoff Lindsey, *English After RP*（p.93）にも言及がある。

> Many younger speakers of SSB now use schwa before vowels as well as consonants, …
>
> | | |
> |---|---|
> | *to address* | tə[?]əˈdres |
> | *the address* | ðə[?]əˈdres |
>
> (This pattern is more established in America, and perhaps in Scotland than in SSB.)

但し、英語母語話者は、母音が重なるのを嫌うので、中間に、いわば「音のない子音」── 声門閉鎖音 /ʔ/ ── を介入させて、それを回避する。

　　　　　注：SSB: Southern Standard British の略。ロンドンを中心とする南部の
　　　　　　　middle and upper-middle class の人びとの発音を指す。

課題 32　　What is Mary doing?

What is Mary doing?

She is taking things from a drawer.

C
What is the girl doing?

　いつも言うように、英語のイントネーションを習得する第一歩は、文中のどの語を最も強調して発音するかを見極めることである。その際、context（前後関係、文脈）が大きく関わってくる。しかし、いちおう基本的規則があって、通例、文中の末尾にある内容語が最も強調されるというものである。換言すれば、その語が核強勢を受ける。但し、「強調される」の意味は、決して「強く（loudly）」というのではない。むしろ、それよりも「高く（higher pitch）」かつ「長く（longer）」のほうが重要である。

　「通例」という予防線を張ったのは、左図（EP p.77）中の What is Mary doing? が、基本的規則から逸脱するからである。この WH 疑問文は、前提条件が無い all-new sentence であるので、doing が最も強調され —— 核強勢を受け —— 高く、長く発音されると思いきや、実際には、そうとはならずに文の中間に位置する Mary が最も目立って発音される。実際、Richards の LP レコード版、洋販の CD，IBC 版の CD では、一致して 'What is ↘Mary doing? となり、Mar- で声（pitch）が他の語よりも一段高くなっている。一方、右図（EP p.117）中の What is the girl doing? では、三者とも末尾の内容語 do(ing) に核強勢が来ている。なぜ両者のイントネーションに違いがあるのか。疑問を解く鍵は、名詞優先主義（noun preference）である。つまり、<u>新情報（初出）の名詞は、文中で優先的に核強勢を受ける</u>。この WH 疑問文では、Mary という名詞は、「藪から棒に」発せられる初出の名詞であり、同じく初出の動詞の強勢を抑えて、核強勢を受ける。一方、右図の the girl は既知情報と見なされている。SUPRAS のメンバーが、下記のように明解な説明をしている。

- When we say that we need to stress the new information, it's logical to think, "Hmmm, this is the first time I'm saying this sentence, so it's all new information. I'd rather stress every word." Well, not quite. In standard

English, we consider that the nouns carry the weight of a sentence, when all else is equal. Although the verb carries important information, it does not receive the primary stress of a first-time noun.

さらに、Wells の解説は、もっと具体性がある。

- We put nucleus on a noun where possible, in preference to other word classes. This is seen in various constructions which involve having a verb at the end of a sentence or clause. A final verb is usually deaccented, and the nucleus goes on a preceding noun.

名詞優先主義の原理は、実に便利な規則である。他の多くの構文にも適用できる。以下の文では、下線部で声の高さが急激に変動し、他の語よりも長くなり、その後は下降に転じる。その際、声の大きさ（loudness）は必ずしも重要ではない。

a. Watch out! There's a ↘car coming.　　（There's a ˈcar ↘coming. はあり得ない）
b. There's a ↘man at the door.　　（There's a ˈman at the ↘door. はあり得ない。）
c. So, ˈhow did the ↘test go?　　（test は初出なので新情報である。）
d. By the day, ˈwhere does Mr. ↘Date live?
e. ˈHow (l)many ↘brothers do you have?
f. Excuse me. ˈWhat ↘time do you have?
g. This is a dog. ˈWhich ↘parts of the dog do you see?
h. ˈThat's a ˈnice ↘hat you're wearing.
i. Oh, dear! The ↘clock has stopped.
j. Sorry to be late. The ↘train was late.
k. The ↘phone's ringing.
l. The ↘wind came. My ˈhat (l)went ↘up.

d
This is a dog.

Which parts of the dog do you see?

ここで注意するべきことは、名詞が定冠詞を伴っているからと言って、既に文脈中にある既知情報とは限らないということである。発話時点で、初めて場面に登場する名詞（first-time noun）は、全て新情報の扱いになる。

The wind came. My hat went up.
When the wind came, my hat went up.

課題 32　　　What is Mary doing?

一方、以下の対話中の a bus は、ほとんど既知情報と言えるだろう。

　A: Excuse me. Which bus goes to the Palace Theater?
　B: The Palace Theater?
　A: Yes.
　B: Take bus no. 104. It stops over there. <u>A bus arrives every ten minutes.</u>
New Horizon 2（現行）: p.79

もし A bus arrives. が event sentence ならば、「突然、1 台のバスが現れる」という出来事文になる。しかし、この対話では、「バスが来る」のは a routine (scheduled) arrival である。バスという概念は、話し手と聞き手の間で共有されている。従って、

　A ˈbus ar ↘↗ rives | ˈevery ⁽ˡ⁾ten ↘ minutes.

課題 33　　**Yes-no question** のイントネーション

　英語の教員にとって最低限必要なことは、核強勢についての基本的知識である。これは、いわば、英語のイントネーションという山に登る登山口である。核強勢を受ける語は、話し手が聞き手の注意を最も引き付けたい箇所であるので、最も強調して発音される。核強勢では、3つの要素が作用して「際立たせ」効果を生む。即ち、音の相対的な高さ（pitch）の変化、音の長さ、音の大きさ（loudness）によって、核強勢を表したり、或いは、聞き手がそれを感じとる。

　今回は、Yes-No 疑問文に関することである。日本人は、各音節の長さがほぼ同じであり、音の大きさも同じとすれば、<u>音の高さによって核強勢を感じる傾向</u>がある。そのために、英語の Yes-No 疑問文を聞いた時に、<u>音が最も高い音節に核強勢があると誤解してしまう</u>。例えば

 a.　Did you ˈhave ↗ <u>fun</u> today?
 b.　Have they ˈleft ↗ <u>home</u> yet?
 c.　Can you ˈhelp me with to ˈmorrow's ↗ <u>math</u> homework?

各文では、それぞれ fun, home, math が核強勢を受けるが、多くの学習者は、-day, yet, -work に核強勢が来ると勘違いする。また、自分で発音する時も、それらを強調してしまう。単に pitch が一番高いだけなのに、そこを高く・強く発音してしまう。このことを渡辺和幸（1988）が実験により立証している。

 (1)　They say that MEAT is very expensive.

という発話で、meat が最も重要な語と見なされ、かつ、meat がこの文で最も高い pitch を帯びている場合には、日本語の際に用いているストラテジーで正しく話し手の意図を把握できるが、

 (2)　Can you come to DINner tomorrow?

のような上昇調を帯びた文では、dinner が最も重要な語であるが、tomorrow の方がピッチが高くなっているために、日本語話者にとっては tomorrow が強いと感じる傾向が強い。実際、大学生120名の内、47名がこの語が最も強いと感じており、dinner が最も強いとした44名を上回った。ちなみに、実験に参加したオーストラリアの大学生にはそのような傾向は認められない。このようなケースでは、英語話者は dinner で始まるピッチ変化に、より強く反応するのである。

   『英語のリズム・イントネーションの指導』（大修館 1994:3）

課題 33　Yes-no question のイントネーション

以上からも明らかなように、din- を起点とした声の高さの目だった変動（上昇調）は、核音節内で完結しないで、それ以降の全ての音節（-ner tomorrow）にまで及ぶ。従って、文強勢をもたない音節であっても、最後の音節が最も高い pitch をもつ。例えば、

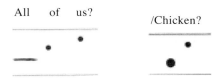

これらの場合、核強勢は all と chick- に来るが、最も目立って聞こえるのは us と -en である。一方、Are you all right? Can you speak French? では、問題は起こらない。以下でも、morning が音調単位中で最も高いが、核強勢は speak に来る。

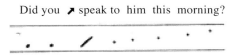

なお、Yes-no 疑問文が下降調で発せられるケースがある。典型的なものは、同じ質問が繰り返される場合である。insistence のニュアンスがある。

a. A: Do you play chess?
　　B: Pardon?
　　A: I ˈsaid, do you ˈplay ↘chess?

b. A: Do you like me?
　　B: You're cute.
　　A: I know that. But do you ↘like me?

c. A: Hey, Norman? Are you afˈraid of ↗dying?
　　B: What?
　　A: Are you afˈraid to ↘die?

課題 34　　　**Thank you.** のイントネーションの諸相

　日本人英語学習者は、Thank you. には感謝以外に様々な意味合いがあることには不案内であろう。イントネーション次第では、感謝とは正反対の意味になることがある。例えば、皮肉であったり、不機嫌を表すにも Thank you が用いられることがある。

a. Sales assistant: Hi. May I help you?
　　Shopper: I'm just looking around, *thank you*.
b. Check-out counter woman: That'll be 5 dollars 45 cents, *thank you*.
c. A: Happy birthday, John! Here's a little something for you.
　　B: Oh, *thank you*.
d. Man: Cathy, what did you do last weekend?
　　Woman: Leave my private life alone, *thank you*.
e. A: I feel like having eggs for breakfast today.
　　B: But I've already made rice and *miso* soup.
　　A: You can eat them, but I'm going to have eggs.
　　B: Well, *thanks a* lot. That's the last time I make breakfast for you.
f. A: Weren't you driving under the influence of alcohol the other day?
　　　According to the law...
　　B: No, I wasn't. And I know the law very well, *thank you*.

これらのうち、a, b, c は相手に対して（軽重の差があるが）感謝の気持ちを、一方、d, e, f は苛立ちや不満の気持ちを述べている。なお、d は、I'll thank you to do... という慣用表現で換言できる。

　I'll thank you to leave my private life alone.
　I'll thank you to mind your own business.

また、e. の場合は、

　I'll thank you for a bit of thoughtfulness / courtesy.

なお、I'll thank you... の定義は以下のとおりである。

　"used to tell someone in an angry way not to do something because it is annoying you."
　　　　　　　　　　　　Longman Dictionary of Contemporary English

　さて、上記の例文中の Thank you. のイントネーションはどうなるだろう。

課題 34　　Thank you. のイントネーションの諸相

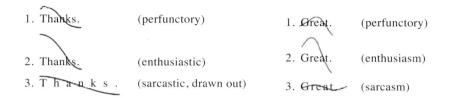

1 は、いわば事務的な言い方であるに対して、2 は、心からの感謝である。3 は皮肉で、声を少し伸ばし加減で言う。なお、これらのイントネーションはすべて下降調であるが、声域（専門語では key とか pitch range と呼ばれる）に差がある。例文中で言えば、1 は、例文中 a と b に用いられるであろう。2 は c に、また、3 はその他に適切であろう。What a beautiful day! も、1 のようなイントネーションでは淡々とした感情を、2 のようなイントネーションでは高ぶった感情を表す。また、3 のようなイントネーション（狭い声域で引き伸ばす）では sarcasm（皮肉）の意味があり、例えば、窓から悪天候の空を見上げながら、"Great." と皮肉る言い方と同じである。

> Speakers can use the pitch of their voice to send a variety of messages because it helps express intentions. Everyone has his or her own normal pitch range. In ordinary speech, we usually keep within the lower part of our pitch range, but if we want to express stronger feelings or involvement, one of the signals we use is extra pitch height.
>
> 　　　　　　　　　　　　Rogerson & Gilbert, *Speaking Clearly* (1990:64)

以上のイントネーションのほかに、他のパターンもある。Daniel Jones 著の *The Pronunciation of English*（1958:314-315）からの例を紹介しておこう。

1067, *Thank you* is sometimes pronounced with a rising intonation (Tune 2) and sometimes with a falling intonation (Tune 1). When a person performs a customary service, the acknowledgement seems to be said more usually with the rising intonation, thus:

ˈθæŋk ju.

But in acknowledging an unexpected favour the falling intonation seems more usual, thus:

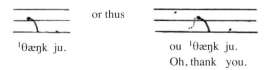

ˈθæŋk ju.　　　　　　ou ˈθæŋk ju.
　　　　　　　　　　　Oh, thank you.

1068, *Thank you* with rising intonation is often reduced to ˈŋkju or kju, thus:

ˈŋkju   or   kju

Thank you with a falling intonation is not generally reduced in this way.

以上のほかに、O'Connor & Arnold が Terrace と呼ぶ平坦調がある。

  A: I've brought your hammer.

  B: ˈThank ➡ you! (p.89)

これは、routine, businesslike な言い方である。

　参考までに述べると、イギリスでは Cheers. とか Ta. ということばをしばしば聞く。これは、上の例 1067 にあるように customary service に対する謝辞である。スーパーのレジやバスを下車する場面でよく使われている。そのイントネーションは、平坦調、または低上昇調が多い。

課題 35　　　不定代名詞の強勢

今回、話題にするのは、不定代名詞の強勢の有無である。Kingdon によれば、不定代名詞は、主語の場合は文強勢を受ける。

The noun-like compounds *somebody*, *someone*, *something*, *anybody*, *anyone* and *anything* are stressed when they are **subjects**.

　　　ˈ*Somebody* must have \lost it.　　　ˈ*Something* \fell just then.

　　　Has ˈ*anything* been /done for it?　　Has ˈ*anyone* seen the /dog?

一方、目的語の場合は文強勢を受けない。

　　　They are usually unstressed when they are **objects**:

　　　I've \seen *someone* about it.　　　You must \have *something* else.

　　　Have you /done *anything* yet?　　　Did you /meet *anybody* there?

　　　　　　　　The Groundwork of English Intonation (1958:177-178)

(i) anything/anybody について

映画 *The Sound of Music* には以下のようなセリフがある。

Maria:　　Now, let's put it all together –

Children:　♫♪ So do la fa mi do re, so do la ti do re do! ♪♫

Brigitta:　But it doesn't mean anything.

Maria:　　So we put in words – one word for every note.

　　　　　When you know the notes to sing,

　　　　　You can sing almost anything.

下線部の強勢配置を示すと、

Brigitta: But it ˈdoesn't ↘ mean anything.

Maria: you can ˈsing almost ↘ anything.

多くの日本人学習者は、恐らく doesn't と anything を強調するだろう。しかし、話者の意図が文を否定することであっても、否定語の後に位置する新情報の内容語 ── mean ── を無視してはいけない。

a.　A: Jack's manners aren't good.

　　B: In what way? I ˈhaven't ↘ noticed anything.

b.　A: What was that?

　　B: I ˈdidn't ↘ hear anything.

c.　I ˈdidn't ↘ see anybody there.

ただし、否定文での anything と anybody は、しばしば上昇調で言われる。

  I ˈhaven't ↘ noticed ↗ anything.

  I ˈdidn't ↘ hear ↗ anything.

  I ˈdidn't ↘ see ↗ anybody.

その理由は、それらが some less important but not completely negligible idea（課題14参照）であると見なされているからである。また、目的語 anything が「何でも」という意味の場合は、上記の You can sing almost anything. と同様に強勢を受ける。

  I'm so hungry. I could ˈeat ↘ anything.

  Say something. ˈSay ↘ anything.

また、強調の場合にも、強勢がある。

  I ˈhaven't [1]eaten ↘ anything yet.

  He ˈdoesn't [1]lend his ˈcar to ↘ anybody.

(ii) something/somebody について

目的語の場合、通常、強勢を受けない。

 a. A: What's wrong?

   B: I have a headache.

   A: You should ↘ take something. (= some medicine)

 b. A: Oh, it's you, Sabrina.

   B: Hello, David.

   A: I ↘ thought I ↗ heard something.

 c. I can't keep it quiet any longer. I've just ˈgot to ↘ tell somebody.

また、話し言葉の or something/somebody は文末では文強勢を受けない。

  His name is ↗ Jimmy, or ↘ Billy, or something.

  Stop bothering me! ˈAsk ↘ Kate or somebody.

但し強調の場合には、強勢がある。

  A: What's wrong?

  B: I ˈthought I ↘ saw someone.

  A: But there's no one at the door.

  B: I'm ˈsure I saw ↘ someone.

(iii) 疑似的 event sentence

event sentence は、初出の名詞主語と初出の述部だけで成り立ち、突発的

課題 35　不定代名詞の強勢

な出来事 — misfortune, accident, (dis)appearance — を告げる。また、名詞主語が核強勢を受ける。実は、不定代名詞も初出の名詞主語と同じ扱いになることがある。

a.　A: ↘Nobody turned up.

　　B: How strange!

b.　A: Hullo, Susan. Sorry to be late.

　　B: What's been keeping you so long?

　　A: I had a bit of trouble with the car. ↘Everything went wrong.

c.　A: We are in trouble.

　　B: Yeah. ↘Anything can happen.

課題 36　　『千の風になって』

Do Not Stand At My Grave And Weep は、講釈するのが野暮とも言える有名な詩である。

　　Do not stand at my grave and weep;
　　I'm not there, I do not sleep.
　　I am a thousand winds that blow.
　　　　（中略）
　　I am the soft stars that shine at night.
　　Do not stand at my grave and cry;
　　I am not there, I did not die.

私の手元には、4ヶ国の英語のネイテイブ・スピーカーによる朗読 CD がある。The University of Queensland の学生 Ms. J（オーストラリア人）、私の元職場の教員 Ms. H（スコットランド系イギリス人）、友人の大学教授 Mr. R（アメリカ人）、Mr. John Wells（イギリス人）による朗読である。彼らの朗読中に聞かれる強勢配置とイントネーションの主な相違点を紹介しよう。

1. 'Do not 'stand... ●●● / Do 'not 'stand... ●●● という2種類の強勢パターンがある。前者は poetry reading に相応しい強弱リズム（stress timing）になっていて more rhythmical であり、後者は more prosaic（散文的）な発音である。この件について、以前に Jack Windsor Lewis にメール送り確認を求めたことがある。Lewis の回答は PhonetiBlog（2009年8月5日）中で紹介された。

> My reply is: Yes, the former stressing sounds like verse and the latter perhaps less so. But they are both rhetorical or at least non-conversational in their avoidance of the normal contracted pronunciation ***Don't*** of ordinary talk. The second, if it were not obviously poetic, could suggest, because of the special stress on *not*, an impatient prohibition of what's being done. There really isn't anything very significant in the different colleagues' preferences.

4人の朗読で強勢配置が違っていても、特にそれに意味があるわけではないという回答である。会話体では短縮形 don't となるが、もし会話中で、Do not stand... と言えば、苛立った（impatient）言い方になるということ

課題 36　『千の風になって』

である（課題 54 参照）。なお、'Do not 'stand ●●●と読んでいるのは Mr. Wells と Ms. H である。また、2 人は I 'do not 'sleep. と言っている。一方、I do 'not 'sleep. は Mr. R と Ms. J の発音である。このタイプの否定文は EP Book 1（p. 41）にもあるので少し解説をしておこう。

　　　My eyes are open. I see. Her eyes are shut. She does not see.

ここでは I ' see. との対比として、' She does 'not see. である。しかし、もし前提となる文脈もなく藪から棒に My eyes are shut. I do not see. と言う場合、

　① リズム重視では I 'do not 'see. となる。一方、

　② 散文的な発音では I do 'not 'see. である。

しかし、Lewis が言うように do not see は non-conversational であり、ordinary talk では I 'don't 'see. が一般的である。

②では強勢音節が連続するのに対して、①は●●●●となり、英語の stress timing に乗って語呂がよい。そう言えば、語呂のよさでは a half hour や a half dozen よりも half an hour, half a dozen のほうが勝る。また、many days よりも many a day（old fashioned）のほうが語呂がよい。many days の語順でも中間に無強勢があり、強勢音節どうしの衝突は起らないが、余分の無強勢音節があるほうが余裕をもって stress timing に乗せることができる（p.78 参照）。あの有名な Hamlet のセリフにおいて、stress timing 重視型では

　　　To 'be or 'not to 'be; that 'is the 'question.

また、『十二夜』（*Twelfth Night*）には、If music be the food of love, play on. というセリフがある。これは、恋に悩む主人公が、学士の奏でる調べを聞きながら口にする言葉である。リズム重視で発音すると、If 'music 'be the 'food of 'love, play 'on. となる。

EP（p.19）には以下の文がある。

　　　He is giving his hat to the man. He gave it to the man.

　　　He gave it to him.

最後の文は、普通、He 'gave it to him. という強勢配置になるけれども、stress timing に乗せる方法として、弱形 /tə/ を強形 /tuː/ に換えて発音することも妥当である。即ち、He 'gave it 'to him.

2. 英語の詩では、しばしば「韻を踏む」（rhyme）という言い方をする。韻に

123

は2種類あって、「脚韻」（rhyme）と「頭韻」（alliteration）である。『千の風になって』では、脚韻を踏んでいる箇所が多い。具体的には weep/sleep；blow/snow；grain/rain；hush/rush；flight/night；cry/die である。なお、rhyme の定義について

 If two words or two lines of poetry rhyme, they end with the same sound, including a vowel. *Hat* rhymes with *cat*.
        Longman Dictionary of Contemporary English

一方、頭韻を踏むのは1箇所で、*soft* と *stars* は語頭の [s] を共有している。類例として Donald Duck, Mickey Mouse, Minnie Mouse, King Kong, Coca-Cola, green as grass, time and tide wait for no man. なども頭韻を踏んでいる。

課題 37　　　**than** の弱形 **vs.** 強形

English Through Pictures Book 2 には以下の箇所がある。これらの文を normal fast tempo で言う時は 1 つの音調単位になり、一方、slower and more deliberate tempo では 2 つの音調単位になり、各単位に核強勢がある。

> This line
> ─────────
> 　　is longer than
> 　　　　this line.
> ─────────
>
> The time between three and four is shorter than the time between three and five.
>
> One hour is a shorter time than two hours.

一気読み（a single tone unit）では、

　ˈThis ˈline is ˈlonger *than* this line. [ðən]

　ˈOne ˈhour is a ˈshorter time than two hours. [ðən]

一方、slower and more deliberate speech では、どこで区切るかによって、than が強形であるか、弱形であるかが違ってくる。

　ˈThis ˈline is longer | *than* this line. [ðən]

　ˈThis ˈline is longer *than* | this line. [ðæn]

つまり、前置詞と同じように、than も休止の直前では強形 [ðæn] になる。

同様にして

　ˈOne ˈhour is a ˈshorter time | *than* ˈtwo hours. [ðən]

　ˈOne ˈhour is a ˈshorter time *than* | ˈtwo hours. [ðæn]

以下の文も 1 つの音調単位で発音するのは無理だろう。

　The time between three and four is shorter | *than* the time between three and five. [ðən]

　The time between three and four is shorter *than* | the time between three and five. [ðæn]

Wells の phonetic blog には、以下のような強形 [ðæn] の例が挙げられている。

　　a.　Who are you bigger *than*?
　　b.　Who is Mary younger *than*?

  c. A mouse is something that an elephant is <u>bigger</u> *than*. (Sept. 7, 2011)

 基本的には、connected speech 中では than は弱形発音 [ðən], [ðn] になる。日本人の多くは、いつも強形発音をしているので、ネーティブ・スピーカーの言っていることを聞き逃すことがあるだろう。特に、この語は fast and casual speech では更に弱化してしまう。例えば、better than は *better'n* と聞こえることもある。それは、右の商品ラベルにも表れている。better than peanut butter は *better'n* peanut butter となっている。同様にして more than も *more'n* と発音されることがある。

以下の比較構文の区切りについて、アメリカ人大学教授に確認をした。彼からの返信を紹介しよう。

 (a) 1. England is a bit larger than | Scotland.

   2. John is much taller than | his younger brother.

 (b) 1. England is a bit larger | than Scotland.

   2. John is much taller than | his younger brother.

"I would agree with you that the strong form of "than" /ðæn/ would be used in all of the above sentences, particularly when "than" precedes the break as in (a1) and (a2). However, if for some reason the speaker intentionally pronounced "than Scotland" very rapidly after the break in (b1), "than" might be reduced to /ðən/ since the comparison has already been set up by "larger" and we know that an object of comparison ("Scotland") must follow, so "than" must appear as a function word before that object.

 蛇足になるが、英語のネーティブ・スピーカーの間では、then と than との混同があって、than と書くべきところ then となるケースがある。以下は、先ほどの blog が出典である。

  "Look at this headline from Saturday's on-line Liverpool Echo. Can you see anything wrong?

    Exclusive Steven Gerrard interview: I'm feeling

    better *then* ever, says Liverpool FC skipper

Yes, *then* ought to be *than*. There are plenty of other examples to be found on the web. In speech, the word *than* is almost always pronounced in its weak form ðən

課題 37　　than の弱形 vs. 強形

　　　　betə ðən ˈevə (better than ever)
　　　　ˈmɔː ðən ju kʊd biˈliːv (more than you could believe)
It is difficult to envisage a context in which one would want to accent it, thereby triggering the **strong form**."

課題 38　　音調単位の区切り

　1つの文をどこで区切るかが今回のテーマである。一般には、短い文は、1つの音調単位を構成することは容易に想像がつく。しかし、そう短絡的に考えられないこともある。発話の意図 ― 話者の態度 ― によっては、それが2つ、或いは、それ以上の音調単位に区切られることもある。例えば、同じ発話を少なくとも以下のように分割することが可能である。

　　　We ˈdonʼt ˈknow ǀ ˈwho she is.
　　　ˈWe ǀ ˈdonʼt ˈknow ˈwho she is.
　　　We ˈdonʼt ǀ ˈknow ˈwho she is.
　　　ˈWe ǀ ˈdonʼt ˈknow ǀ ˈwho she is.

このように短い文を2つ、または3つの音調単位に分割するときは、slower and more deliberate tempo になる。話者は、音調単位中で重要と考える語を強調する。別の見方をすれば、それは、話し手が聞き手の注意を集中させようとする語である。その際、各区切り（音調単位）の末尾の語が核強勢を受ける。

　映画『恋人たちの予感』（*When Harry Met Sally...*）で、Harry は、執拗に Sally に私生活のことを尋ねる。

　　　Harry:　Are you seeing anybody?
　　　Sally:　Harry…
　　　Harry:　What?
　　　Sally:　I donʼt want to talk about it.
　　　Harry:　Why not?
　　　Sally:　ˈI ǀ ˈdonʼt ǀ ˈwant ǀ to ˈtalk ǀ aˈbout it!

［素晴らしい国歌演奏の後で］
　　ˈHave /youǀ ˈever /heardǀ ∨ ˈsuch a ∨ ˈmarvelousǀ ↘ ˈanthem?

　　　　　　　　　　　　　　　　　　　　　　　Wells (2006:192)

　GDM のことに話題を移そう。*English Through Pictures* の朗読資料やワークショップでの模擬授業デモでは、発音が slower and more deliberate tempo なので、文が区切られて ― 音調単位に分けられて ― いる。例えば、

　　　He will ˈtake his hat ǀ[1] off the table.
　　　He is taking it ǀ[1] off the table.
　　　He will ˈput his hat ǀ[1] on his head.

課題 38　　音調単位の区切り

　　He is |putting his hat | ⁽¹⁾on his head.
この場合も、各音調単位の末尾の内容語が核強勢を受ける。なお、各文の後半の副詞句では、前置詞 off と on は文強勢を受けることがある。その理由は、英語のリズムの基調となっている stress timing（強勢拍）の影響により、できるだけ早く強勢音節を確保しようとするからである。
 (i) 区切りが新情報と既知情報とを区別する

　　前者は下降調で、後者は上昇調または下降・上昇調で言われる。ここでは、特に新情報（初出）の名詞主語を採り上げる。名詞主語は、独自の音調単位となるので直後に区切りができる。その際、音調単位は下降調、または、下降上昇調になる。前者は、名詞主語が初出であり、後者は、それが既知内容の場合である。
 ① 名詞主語が新情報の場合
　a. A |big, ⁽¹⁾old ↘ tree | stands by a road near the city of Hiroshima. One summer night | the ↘↗ tree | heard a lullaby. A ↘ mother | was singing to her little girl under the tree.　　　*New Horizon* 3（旧版）
　b. Have you heard the news? The ↘ Joneses | have got a new car.
　c. The ↘ snow | generally comes early in October.

```
                                              to
         snow                    ear
                generally comes      ly  in Oc
   The                                         ber.
```
　　　　　　　　　　　　　　　　Bolinger, *Intonation* (1972:23)
　d. A: What happened?
　　 B: Your ↘ brother | broke his leg.

```
            bró              lé
   Your
              ther broke his    g.
```

 ② 名詞主語が既に文脈に存在するとき、
　a. A: What have your parents been doing recently?
　　 B: My ↘↗ parents | have been to England.
　b. A: What happened to my brother?
　　 B: Your ↘↗ brother | broke his leg.

```
                    bró              lé
        Your
                  th e r  broke his    g.
```
                               Bolinger, *Intonation and Its Parts* (1986:182)

(ii) 区切りが意味を区別する

   a. The gold watch, | which I bought in Geneva, | keeps good time.
      （唯一の時計）

      The gold watch which I bought in Geneva, | keeps good time.
      （複数の中の1つ）

   b. Would you like tea | or coffee?　　（上昇＋下降）

      Would you like tea or coffee (or something)?　　（上昇調）

   c. [He was born and grew up in Singapore.]

      He speaks English naturally. (= fluently)

      He speaks English, | naturally. (= of course)

   d. The professor, said the students, | asked many questions.

      The professor said | the students asked many questions.

   e. [Where's Sally today?]

      She said | she had a headache. (I doubt it.)

      She said she had a headache. (ordinary type)

   f. He died a happy man.
      （主格補語：幸せに生涯を終えた。He ˈdied a ˈhappy ↘ man）

      He died | a happy man.
      （同格：あの幸せな男は死んだ。He ↘ died, | a ˈhappy ↗ man.）

   g. He came to hear about it.
      （it happened by chance：たまたま～するようになった）

      He came | to hear about it.
      （for a purpose：するために：He ↘↗ came | to ↘ hear about it.）

   h. You should wake up and smell the coffee.
      （continuous single action；idiom：現実を直視せよ）

      You should wake up | and smell the coffee.
      （two separate actions, literal meaning）

課題 39　　　代名詞の対比用法

EP Book One には、以下の文がある。

　They are at the window together.
　① She is with him at the window.
　② He is with her at the window.　(p. 38)

下線部①はどのようなイントネーションで言うのが適切だろうか。特に、どの語が文強勢を受けるだろうか。まず、at the window は反復表現なので、window には文強勢はなく、目立った pitch（声の高低）変化が起こらない。文脈から判断すると、with が最も重要な語であるから、ここに核強勢が来て pitch の際立った（prominent）の変動が起こる。つまり、pitch がいったん高くなり下降調に向かう。その下降方向を win- が引き継ぐ。

　　She is ↘with him at the window.

なお、window は文強勢を受けないが、語強勢（辞書に表記されている強勢）はある。次に②では、①中の主語と前置詞の目的語とが入れ替わっており、それはイントネーションに反映される。具体的には、入れ替わった語（He と her）に文強勢を置く。

　　ˈHe is with ↘her at the window.

her を起点として pitch はいったん高くなり下降調に向かい、window がそれを引き継ぐ。さらに、EP には以下の文もある。

　They went from the window. She went with him and he went with her. (p.39)

　　ˈShe went with ↘↗him ǀ and ˈhe went with ↘her.

更には、以下のような対比もある。

　She does not see. ˈI see ↘her. ˈShe does ˈnot see ↘me.
　What does she see? She sees me. ˈI see ↘her.　(p.41)

文献からの例を少し紹介しよう。

　a.　ˈJohn insulted <u>Mary</u>, and then ˈ*she insulted <u>him</u>*.
　　　　　　　　　　　　　　　(adapted from S. Schmerling 1973:72)
　b.　It's not that ˈAlan doesn't like <u>Kate</u>: ˈ*She can't stand <u>him</u>*.
　　　　　　　　　　　　　　　(adapted from R. Knowles 1987:154)
　　　注：文脈では、*doesn't like* と *can't stand* とは同義語であると考えられる。

b. ˈBill threatened <u>Jim</u> and then ˈhe hit <u>him</u>.　(= Jim hit Bill.)

この場合、代名詞主語 he に文強勢を置くことによって、それが指し示す人（referent）は、最初の文の主語 Bill とは異なるというシグナルを伝えている。

> "But by accenting the subject pronoun we signal that its referent is not the same as the subject of the previous verb. Accenting ***he*** means that there is a change of subject, in this case from ***Bill*** to ***Jim***. Likewise, accenting ***him*** indicates that the object of ***hit*** is different from the object of ***threatened***."　　　　　　(2006:239)

しかし、よく考えてみると、主語代名詞と目的語の両方に文強勢を置かなくとも、どちらか1つを強調するだけで、所期の目的は果たせる。その際は、後方の語に文強勢（核強勢）を置く。文頭よりも文末の文強勢のほうが、いわば体操選手の"着地のフィニッシュ"のように、効果的（last seen (heard), best noted）であると言えるだろう。実際、I see her. She does not see her. でも、音声資料で主語（I と she）に強勢を置かない朗読がある。

(i) 主語と目的語の双方に文強勢を置くケース

  a. A: You know, the first time we met, I really didn't like you that much.
     B: ˈ*I didn't like <u>you</u>*.

  b. A: Ever since Rachel met Steve the other day, she hasn't stopped talking about him. I don't know why she ever broke up with him.
     B: I ˈthought ˈ*he broke up with <u>her</u>*.

  c. A: Look up there!
     B: Where?
     A: There in the trees! Ah, I hate bats! They're going to fly in my hair.
     B: Don't worry. ˈ*Bats are* ˈ*more af*ˈ*raid of <u>you</u>* | *than* ˈ*you are of <u>them</u>*.

(ii) 片方（目的語）にのみ文強勢を置くケース

  a. A: Honey, I love you.
     B: *And I love <u>you</u>*.

  b. A: You're entirely too wrapped up with Steve.
     B: I ˈ<u>love</u> him and *he loves <u>me</u>*.

  c. I ˈsee the ˈ<u>moon</u> and *the moon sees <u>me</u>*.

  d. I feel sorry for him. He's in love with her, but she's ˈ*not in love with <u>him</u>*.

課題 40　　EPにおける対比強勢の諸相

　English Through Pictures（EP）中の文は、特定の場面（situation）を描写しているので、それに即したイントネーションで言う必要がある。その際、最も重要なことは、どの語を最も強調して ── 換言すれば、<u>どの語に核強勢を置いて</u> ── 発音するかである。日本語の話し言葉では、普段、そのようなことはほとんど意識しない。

　英語学習では、このような日本語と英語とのギャップが間違いの要因になる。以下の英文は、SUPRASの会員から私に宛てた公開質問である。

　　[A story about a Japanese girl who thinks she is calling her mother but accidentally dials the number of her best friend and is really calling her best friend's mother]

　　　"I didn't know it was her MOTHER! I thought it was my MOTHER!"

このようなエラーは、多くの日本人学習者に見られる。正しくは、

　　　I didn't know it was HER mother! I thought it was MY mother!

質問者は言う。

　　　"Tami, is there anything in Japanese grammar/intonation/pragmatics that would explain this error? The person is otherwise rather advanced in English..." (Feb. 28, 2007)

私の返信内容は、ここでは割愛するが、容易に推察できるだろう。

　さて、<u>EPでは、対比強勢</u>が頻出する。そこでは、相互に関連した文が、様々なsituationに出てくるので、各文中で焦点が置かれる語 ── 核強勢を受ける語 ── が中立的な位置である文末ではなく、もっと前の方に移動することがある。以下は、絵と文から<u>予想できる</u>文強勢配置とイントネーションである。

a.　ˈThis is my ↘hat. ˈThat is ↘his hat. (p.12)　　　［my vs. his との対比］

b.　He is taking his hat off his head. His ˈhat is in his ↘hand.
　　It ↘was | on his ↘head. (p. 16)　　　2つの音調単位に分かれる
　　　［is vs. was との対比、及び hand vs. head との対比］

c.　ˈThis is a ↘glass. It is ˈon the ↘table.
　　↘↗Now | the ˈglass is ↘off the table. (p.23)　　　［on vs. off との対比］

d.　ˈWhat is the ↘time? The ˈtime is ↘two.
　　It ↘was | ↘one. It ↘will | be ↘three.　　　［is vs. three; one vs. three］

では、実際に音声資料で聞かれる文強勢とイントネーションはどうであろうか。私の手元にある3つの音声資料を聴いて確かめてみた。その資料とはHarvard 大学の Richards 作成 LP レコード（カセットテープに収録）と、比較的新しい2つの CD 版（Yohan と IBC Publishing）である。例文の a, c, d では3つの資料で一致しているが、b では、Yohan CD だけが was に強勢を置いていない。まるで過去形の Where was his hat? に対する返答のように It was ˈon his ↘head. と言っている。

このような強勢配置のズレは、朗読者の行う情報処理の違いによるものである。つまり It was on his head. では、文脈上で on his head が最も重要な情報であると単純に解釈して言うと head に核強勢が来る。それに対して、状況をもっと深く読み取って was と is との対比も同じく大変重要な語であると解釈するときは、そこも対比強勢（contrastive stress）が来る。従って、文は double contrast を表すことになる。

このような情報の切り取り方の違いによって、1つの文の発音に個人差ができるケースが EP のあちこちに見られる。

e. [His hat is on the table. p.14] He ˈput his ˈhat on his ↘head.
　　It ↘was | on the ↘table. or It was ˈon his ↘head. (p.15)
　　　　　　　　　　　　　　[2つの音調単位に分けているのはテープ資料のみ]

f. I ˈhave a ˈbook in my hand now.
　　It ↘was | on the ↘shelf. or It was ˈon the ↘shelf.
　　　　　　　　　　　　　　[2つの音調単位に分けているのはテープ資料のみ]

今回、3つの音声資料を点検したが、LP（テープ版）のほうが situation をより忠実に反映しており、教材としては断然信頼がおける。一方、CD 版には、イントネーションの理論から見て、時々、少し首をかしげるような朗読がある。朗読者が situation を適切に読み取っていないのではないかと思える。時々、学習者や日本人英語指導者を戸惑わせる箇所がある。

(i) His ˈhat is in his ↘hand. It ↘ˈwas | on his ↘head.
　　He ˈtook his hat ↘off. (p.16)
　　ところが、IBC の CD では既に文脈にある既知内容語 hat に核強勢を置いている。??? He ˈtook his ↘hat off. 情報処理が間違っている。

(ii) My ˈeyes are ↘ˈopen. I ↘ˈsee. ˈHer eyes are ↘shut. (p.41)
　　Yohan CD では Her ˈeyes と言っている。これも解せない。

課題 40　EP における対比強勢の諸相

(iii)　Her ˈeyes are ↘ open. She ↘ sees. They ↘ were | ↘ shut.
　　　She did ↘ not see. She did ˈnot see ↘ me.　(p.41)
　　　IBC の CD では、???She did ˈnot ↘ see me. 不可解。

　日本語は、他者との対比を伝えるのに表意文字で表すことが多く、イントネーションに頼るのは必ずしも必要ではない。例えば、「私なんか（あなたなんか）には分からない」とか、「私の方に誤解がありました」、「ひとの気持ちも知らないで」などと言い、代名詞にアクセントかぶせなくても所期の目的は果たせる。更に、日本人は、場面や敬語に頼って、できるだけ主語や目的語などを省略した話し方をするのに慣れている。英語は、その真逆である。だから、**The** *Tales of Genji* は、『源氏物語』と比べて、はるかに読みやすい。英語の授業で、「代名詞は、他者との対比を示す場合には、文強勢を受ける」と習っても、理屈では理解できるが、そもそも日本人には対比アクセントの認識がはっきりと存在しないので英語では実践力がなかなか身につかない。代名詞だけでなく、前置詞や be 動詞の対比用法にも対応ができないことが多い。その意味で、EP は、これらを実感する格好の教材である。

教室の音声学

課題 41　　暫定的な気持ちを伝えるイントネーション

　英語を書くときに文法が必要なように、英語を話すときにも「音法」が必要である。しかし、イントネーションの音法の学習や指導は、全く手つかずの状態である。日本語では、話し手の態度、焦点、強調、対比などを伝えるのに、漢字をはじめ表意文字で表す範囲が広く、道具立てが揃っているので、必ずしもイントネーションに頼らなくても意志伝達ができる。英語では、文中の特定の箇所— 単語 —にイントネーションを自由自在にかぶせることによって意志伝達をすることが多い。なぜならば、日本語と比べて、英語は、「文字で表現できる」道具立てが乏しいからである。そのため、英語は大きくイントネーションに依存する言語である。このことは、早々と中学校の教科書に見られる。

Mike: Oh, no! My cola!
　　　 I don't have any tissues.
　　　 Do you have any?
Emi:　 No, but <u>I have a handkerchief</u>.
　　　 Here. Use this.

日本人ならほとんど誰もが、下記の文を次のように下降調で言うだろう。

・but I ˈhave a ↘<u>hand</u>kerchief.

・but I can ↘<u>swim</u>.

・but you can ˈsee me in the ↘<u>zoo</u>.

I'm black and white. What am I?
Let's see. Can we find you at school?
No, but you can see me in the zoo.
Are you a bird?
Yes, and I like cold places.
Can you fly?
No, but I can swim.
I got it! Are you a penguin?
Yes, I am.

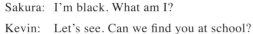

Sakura:　I'm black. What am I?
Kevin:　 Let's see. Can we find you at school?
Sakura:　No, but you can see me in the zoo.
Kevin:　 Are you large?
Sakura:　Yes, I am. I look like a bear.
Kevin:　 Do you live in China?
Sakura:　Yes, I do.
Kevin:　 I got it. You're a panda, aren't you?

課題 41　暫定的な気持ちを伝えるイントネーション

　上記に挙げた 3 例を下降調で言っても不適切とは言えないが、もっと話し手の態度（心理状態）に気を配ったイントネーション（discourse intonation）では、以下のようになる。

　　but I ˈhave a ↘↗<u>hand</u>kerchief.　（実際には ↘<u>hand</u>kerchief ↗）
　　but I can ↘↗<u>swim</u>.
　　but you can ˈsee me at the ↘↗<u>zoo</u>. となる。

問題は、なぜそのような口調になるのか？　その理由は、対比目的であるとも言えるが、むしろ暫定的なニューアンスがあるからである。末尾を少し上昇調で言うことによって、non-final, incomplete の気持ちを伝える。つまり、「ハンカチなら（ば）」、「泳ぐことなら（ば）」、「動物園でなら（ば）」というニューアンスである。以下も、中学校の教科書からの例である。

Nana:　　Let's try *kakizome*.
Maya:　　What's that?
Nana:　　It's a traditional New Year's event.
　　　　　We write our favorite words with a brush.
Jack:　　 Sounds like fun. I can write some *kanji*.
Maya:　　I can't write any kanji. But I can ˈwrite *hira* ↘↗*gana*.
　　　　　　　　　　　　　　　（実際には *hira* ↘ *gana* ↗.）

Ms. Hall:　Do you play soccer?
Taku:　　　Yes, I do. Do you play soccer, Ms. Hall?
Ms. Hall:　No, I don't. But I ˈplay ↘↗<u>basket</u>ball.
　　　　　　　　　　　　　　　（実際には ↘<u>basket</u>ball ↗）

では、以下の下線部はどのようなイントネーションが適切あろうか。

　A: Are you going to be free next week?
　B: Yes, <u>I'm free on Tuesdays</u>.　　（火曜ならば）

このように、質問に対して部分的、または暫定的な返答の場合は、下降・上昇調のイントネーションが用いられる。

　a.　A: Do you have bread and milk for breakfast?
　　　 B: ↘<u>Yes</u>, ↘↗<u>generally</u>.
　b.　A: Do you ever travel abroad?
　　　 B: ↘<u>Yes</u>, ↘↗<u>sometimes</u>.
　c.　A: Do you always get up early in the morning?

B: ¹Not ↘↗ always.
　d.　A: Is he still teaching at school?
　　　B: ↘ Yes, as ¹far as I re ↘↗ member (↘↗ know).

New Crown 2（旧版）にも、以下の例がある。

　　A: Do you speak English?
　　B: A ↘↗ little. (p.10)
　　　Cf. X: Do you ever eat pork?
　　　　　Y_1: ↘ Yes, ↘ always.
　　　　　Y_2: ↘ No, ↘ never (¹hardly ↘ ever).

このようなイントネーションについて、非常に分かり易い指針がある。

　　So if the answer shows 0 or 100 or something very near to 0 or 100, then the intonation falls. But if the answer is somewhere in the middle, we use the fall-rise.　　　　　Ian Thompson, *Intonation Practice* (1981:40)

課題 42　　　句動詞の commands

　句動詞は、イントネーションに大きな影響を与える。句動詞は、通例、double stress を受け、副詞のほうが、より目立って発音されると考えられている。今回は句動詞から成る命令文（commands）を論じる。実際には、下降調よりも、むしろ末尾で上昇調になることが多い。ˈSpeak ↗up. ˈCheer ↗up. 一方、下降調は、文字通り、命令や指示したり、相手の benefit や comfort のために助言したり、指示する場合に使われる。ところが、日本人の英語教員や研究者にも認識されていないように思えるのは、動詞のほうに、より強い強勢があるケースである。例えば、親が、厳しく子どもを躾けるとき、↘Sit still. ↘Mind your manners. また、誰かを叱るとき、You're acting silly. ↘Grow up! また、社会的に優位な立場にある者が、目下に向かって高圧的に命令する。↘Come on, ↘hand it over. ↘Sit down!　かつて、アメリカの中間選挙前の演説で、トランプが、自分を非難するプラカードを振りかざし抗議している若い女性に向かって、↘Get out! ↘Go back to your mommy! と罵っていた。このように、話者が、<u>苛立ちや怒り、高圧的な態度を示すときの command</u> では、核強勢が動詞に来ると考えられる。ここで「考えられる」という言葉を使うのは、以下のような経緯があるからである。この件について、私は、もう 10 年以上も前に海外の研究者たち（SUPRAS—a closed international e-mail list of phoneticians）と意見交換をしたことがある。まず、私の考えに対する 3 つの反論を紹介しよう。

- I'm saying that in an order such as "Shut up!" the verbal element is not stressed, but that the particle must also be stressed and would probably be tonic.　　　　　　　　　　　　　　注：tonic は核強勢と同義である。
- I agree with John — the particle is obligatorily accented. I suggest that some people are misidentifying, say, a high head on *shut* and a low fall on *up* as a tonic on *shut*.
- It is a pattern often heard on angry, insolent, or would-be tough commands... but "catch up" is a two-stress verb, and an accent on "up" is obligatory in this context.

筆者は、このような反論にめげずに、音声学的整合性やコンセンサスには合わないかもしれないが、少なくとも聴覚印象では、動詞のほうが目立って（more prominent) に聞こえると主張し続けた。次々と同調する意見が寄せられた。

- Dear Tami, if it is of any help or comfort to you, I can hear both "GET up!" and "STAND up!" exactly as you do. I do genuinely sympathize with your doubts.
- I think it's pretty common as an expression of impatience or sometimes exasperation. You hear it also with GET out! START over! SHAPE up! and so on. It works with other expressions, too, like GET lost (which in a neutral voice would be get LOST). I hear my scolding maternal voice when I try these out.
- The falling tone can be shifted to the first element of a few expressions when the speaker has really lost patience. We have: SHUT up. Even less polite are the combination of expletives + off: Oh, *** off! The strategy has the advantage of giving full weight to the 'important' word... Surely it can happen with "COME on, Tim. You must know the answer to that!"
- The same would be true in "BE quiet!" "GET outta here!" "GO home!"(said to a dog) & other short commands with strong negative feelings (with accompanying voice quality change).

このような異例の強勢パターンがあることを認めないと、以下のダジャレ（play on words）が分からなくなる。映画 *Pulp Fiction* の中に次のようなセリフがある。

> Three tomatoes are walking down the street, papa tomato, mama tomato and baby tomato. Baby tomato starts lagging behind and papa tomato gets really angry, goes back and squishes him. Says catch up.
>
> 注：¹catch up をトマトを潰す（squish）とケチャップ（¹ketchup）になり、両者は homophone である。

念のために言うが、通常の command では、副詞のほうに目立った強勢（核強勢）がくる。その際も、イントネーションによって、話者の態度の違いがある。花見客が、混雑した通路を進みながら、時々、写真を撮るために立ち止まっていると、

    a. Now ˈmove a ↘long, please. (firm and authoritative)
    b. Now ˈmove a ↗long, please. (routine and friendly)
    c. Now move a ↘↗long, please. (urgent and a warning)

課題 43　　What language do you speak to each other?

　もう10年以上も前の夏、朝鮮中学・高校の英語教員の研修会で講師を務めた。全国から集まった比較的若手の教員30数名が2コマ（90分×2コマ）の講義と演習に参加した。また、東京にある朝鮮大学校外国語学部の教授も参観された。私は、研修内容の素材を朝鮮学校で使用されている共通教科書（中学1, 2, 3年）に絞った。民族系の学校らしく、*Korean Schools in Japan* というタイトルのレッスンには、以下のような内容がある。

Salma:　By the way, when did Koreans come to Japan?
Yong Sil:　Our great-grandparents came over to Japan before 1945. Then Korea was under Japanese rule.
John:　I see.
Yong Sil:　And there were no Korean schools in Japan. After 1945 they built schools for their children.　　（中学2年生教科書）

また、イングランドに征服・併合された結果、母語を捨て、英語使用を強制されたウエールズに関するユニットや、広島の原爆で多くのKoreansが死亡し、平和記念公園にはその犠牲者の碑があるという内容もある。

　さて、標記の文は、教科書にある。どのようなイントネーションで読むのが適切であろうか。文を作るときに必要な文法があるように、英文を読むときにも音法というものがある。それは、grammar of speech とも言える。その中で、最も重要なのは核強勢である。以下の下線部では

A: I'm angry with John.
B: What did he do?
A: <u>He broke my pen.</u>

核強勢は、pen に来る。このように考えると、What language do you speak to each other? でも、文末の other が「文中で最も強調して発音される語」（即ち核強勢）となるはずである。実は、each other は相互代名詞であり、原則的には、文強勢を受けない。

We HELP each other.
They LOVE one another.

help と love を起点として声の高さ（pitch）の際立った変動が起る。その変動とは、下降調のことである。相互代名詞は、それぞれの動詞の下降調の末尾の

低いピッチを受け継ぐだけである。ただし、CD を聞いたときに相互代名詞に語強勢（辞書中で記された強勢）があるが、独自のピッチ変化を伴わないので文強勢を受けるとは考えない。

　では、核強勢を受ける次の候補は speak となり、What language do you SPEAK to each other? となるか。これは、時には妥当な考え方である。ただし、このように発音する場合には、重要な条件、つまり、文脈が絡んでくる。それは、language が既に文脈に存在し、話し手と聞き手との間の共通認識になっていることが必要である。そうでない場合 —— language という概念が突然に文脈に導入された（初出の）場合 —— 、それは核強勢を受けて、What LANguage do you speak to each other? となる。つまり、language（実際には lan-）で大きなピッチの変動が起こり、それ以降の内容語（speak）と相互代名詞は、-guage の末尾の低いピッチを受け継ぐ。ただし、speak, each, other は、低いピッチながらも語強勢はあるので比較的明瞭に聞こえる。このように、新情報の名詞は優先的に核強勢を受ける。なお、Wells の blog (Tuesday, 8 June 2010) には、私との意見交換が紹介されている。

Tami Date wrote to me about a textbook he was reviewing. In one exercise, students were given a printed dialogue that read in part as follows...

Tami asks about nucleus placement in the second line. He thinks, rightly, that the nucleus should go on *language*.

Yet if we apply the rule of thumb that the nucleus goes on the last new lexical item, we would expect it to go on *speak*.

(?) What language do you <u>speak</u> to each other?

Tami defends his view by saying that there is a hierarchy of accentability among lexical words, in which nouns rank first because of their richer semantic value. I'm not sure that I would know how to measure so nebulous a quality as 'semantic value', but <u>Tami is certainly right that nouns tend to be preferred over other parts of speech when we assign the nucleus.</u> I touch on this point in my *English Intonation* book, §3.29.

...a more general tendency: we put the nucleus on a noun where possible, in preference to other word classes. This is seen in various constructions which involve having a verb at the end of a sentence or clause. A final

課題 43　What language do you speak to each other?

verb is usually deaccented, and the nucleus goes on a preceding noun.

ˈHow's the ˈhomework going?

I've ˈstill got an ˈessay to write.

Which ˈbook did you choose?

以下の対話文で初出の名詞 potato と films に注目しよう。

a.　Waiter: Good evening. Can I help you?

　　Customer: Yes. Can I have the steak special, please?

　　Waiter: OK. *ˈWhat* ⁽ˡ⁾*kind of po*ˡ***ta****to do you want?*

　　Customer: Baked, please.

b.　Interviewer: Miss Harrod, a question on everyone's lips, I'm sure.

　　　　ˈHow ⁽ˡ⁾*many* ˈ***films*** *have you appeared in?*

　　G. Harrod: Why does everyone always ask me that?

課題 44　　　end focus 「文末焦点」

　クリントン大統領政権下のある夏、北朝鮮に逮捕・監禁されていたアメリカ人女性記者が、解放後の記者会見で安堵と感激の情を込めて以下のように述べた。

　"We were afraid we would be sent to a hard-labor camp. Then one day we were told that we were going to a meeting. When we entered the room, **we saw standing before us President Clinton**."

太字部は、通常の語順では We saw President Clinton standing before us. となる。女性記者の発言は、語順を組み換えし dramatic effect を狙っている。英語に限らず、たいがいの言語では、情報上で最も重要な項目は文尾に置かれ、そこに「落ち」(punch line) がある。この例に見られるケースは end focus（文末焦点）とか end weight（文末重点）と呼ばれる。

　英語では、自分の意思を効果的に伝えるには end focus は極めて重要である。例えば、「（若い時に）母から料理を教えてもらった」を I learned cooking from my MOTHer. とか I was taught cooking by my MOTHer. と言った場合、要点が「料理（を習った）」であるならば、この2文は、ピント外れになり、所期の目的を達することができない。なぜなら「母」に文末焦点が当たっており、cooking の概念は文中に埋もれているからである。時には、cooking は既知情報である場合もある。従って、正しくは、My mother taught me COOKing. と言わなければいけない。同様にして、「友人からプレゼントをもらった」も I was given a present by my friend. と英訳するのは必ずしも妥当ではない。次は妥当なケースである。

　(Where did these chairs come from?) They were bought by my UNcle.

対照例を示すと

　I sent John a long LETter. ≠ I sent a long letter to JOHN.

　I taught John JapaNESE. ≠ I taught Japanese to JOHN.
　　　　（ある程度習得した）　　　　　（一時的な指導だけ）

授業でよく行われている「書き換え」練習は、要注意である。

　また、「中だるみ」という表現があるように、文頭と文尾とは対照的に、中位は目立たない場所である。

・We tend to favor the two extremes of the sentence (or in longer sentences,

課題44　end focus「文末焦点」

the two extremes of each relatively independent phrase or clause), as if to announce the beginning and the end. There may be intermediate accents, but they are less prominent.

Bolinger, "Around the Edge of Language: Intonation" in *Intonation* (1972:23)

```
         bró                    lé                                              to
Your                                       snow                  ear
             ther broke his        g.  The       generally comes    ly in Oc      ber.
```

上記の2文では、broke と generally comes が、中間の文強勢として強勢が抑制されていることが分かる。

- In **\<writing\>**, you cannot point to important information by using intonation, so you have to rely on ordering and subordination of clauses instead. The general rule is that <u>the most important new information is saved up to the end</u>, comparable to the end-focus principle in **\<speech\>**.

G. Leech & J. Svartvick, *A Communicative Grammar of English* (1994:196)

しかし、英語は、ほぼ語順が定まっていて柔軟性を欠くので、情報的に副次的な語や句、節であっても、それを<u>文末に配置</u>せざるを得ないことがある。その際、イントネーションが、主情報と副次的情報の区別をする。主情報（通例、新情報）は下降調で、副次的情報（通例、既知情報、付加的情報）は（低）上昇になる。

Perhaps we might say that the basic meaning of a falling tone is something like 'major information' or 'primary information'. Correspondingly, the shared general meaning of non-falling tones is something like 'incomplete information', 'minor information', 'secondary information'. We use falls and non-falls together to indicate the structuring of our message, showing what is primary (by a fall) and what is secondary (by a non-falling tone)

John Wells, *English Intonation* (2006:72-73)

以下は、主情報と副次的情報を伴う例である。後者は（低）上昇調になっている。

(i) 反復語や既知情報の語や句は（低）上昇調になる。

a. A: Uh-oh! It's started to rain.
　　B: I ↘ thought it was going to ↗ rain.

b. A: You look a little tired.
　　B: I ↘ am ↗ tired.

c. A: I've got some chocolate here.
　B: Oh good. I ↘ like ↗ choc olate.
d. A: Excuse me. Is Andrea Zuckerman around?
　B: ↘ I am ↗ she.

(ii) 新情報であっても副次的情報（subsidiary information）は（低）上昇調になる。

a. We can ↘ walk there | if there's ↗ time.
b. I'll ↘ ask him | if ↗ necessary.
c. He's ↘ late | as ↗ usual.

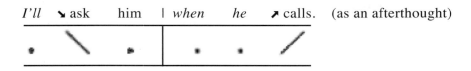

I'll ↘ ask him | *when* he ↗ calls.　(as an afterthought)

課題 45　　　event sentence「出来事文」

EP Book One (p.75) に The wind came. という短い文がある。これは event sentence である。event sentence は、通例、初出の名詞主語と初出の述部だけで成り立つ第 1 文型の文で、misfortune, accident, (dis)appearance を告げる。つまり、突発的な（out-of-the-blue）「出来事」の文である。この強勢パターンはユニークである。なぜなら、核強勢（音調核）が、定番の位置 ── 文中の末尾の内容語 ── ではなく、文頭の名詞主語に来るからである。従って、The ˈwind came となり、述部の強勢は抑えられる。換言すれば、「出来事文」とは、名詞優先主義が典型的に反映された happening を伝える第 1 文型の文である。上記の突風の件では、帽子が飛ばされているという misfortune が起こっている。以下の例も、appearance や misfortune を伝えている。

a. [What's wrong?] The ˈengine won't start.（どうしても始動しない）
b. I'm sorry I'm late. My ˈcar broke down.
c. He's not at school this week. His ˈmother died.
d. [The old pond;] A ˈfrog jumps in.
e. Uh-oh! My ˈwatch stopped.
f. Waiter, there's a ˈfly in my soup.
g. Did you hear the news? There's a ˈstorm coming.
h. The ˈhandle has fallen off.

逆に、My ˈcar $^{(1)}$ broke ˈdown. の場合、車が以前から不調であることが話し手と聞き手の間で共有されていた context での発言である。

論文や著作などで「出来事文」（all-news sentence）が大々的に話題になった契機は、Susan Schmerling, *Aspects of Sentence Stress*（1976）の中で、ˈJohnson died. と ˈTruman ˈdied. の強勢配置の違いが詳細に論じられたことであった。それ以降、あちこちで引用されてきた。先行研究もあったが、Schmerling が火付け役になった。さて、ˈJohnson died. では、彼の突然の死を伝える際の強勢配置である。発話時には、聞き手の意識の中には Johnson の健康状態のことなど存在していなかった、或いは、話者がそのように勝手に判断している。一方、ˈTruman ˈdied. では、Truman 元大統領の病状悪化が国民の意識にあった。

Wells は、第 2 文型（S+V+C）の例を挙げている。

Some event sentences involve an adjective as well as a verb and we again see the noun receiving the nuclear accent, rather than the verb or the adjective.

    Your 'zip's come undone.

    The 'door's open.

Descriptions of the weather count as event sentences of this type:

    It's a funny day; | the 'sun's shining but there's a 'wind springing up.

So do the statements relating to unpleasant bodily sensations:

    My 'arm's hurting.

    My 'nose is all red. (2006: 174-5)

第2文型の他の例を挙げよう。

  a. Hurry up, dear. Your 'toast's getting cold.
  b. There's brown water! The 'pipes are rusty.
  c. I must get home. My 'son's ill.
  d. I'm sorry to be late. The 'train was late.
  e. I just heard that my 'father's dead.

しかし、名詞主語が人（human agent）であり、自主的な行動を告げる場合には、double stress の強勢配置になり、述語動詞に核強勢が来る。

By contrast, if the subject denotes a human agent and the predicate denotes an action over which the subject is likely to have some control, accent on the verb is more likely.（出典不詳）

    My 'brothers are 'wrestling.

    'John 'wept.

    The pro'fessor 'swore.　　（口汚く罵った）

他の例を挙げると

  a. 'Homer (')sometimes 'nods.　　（弘法も筆の誤り）
  b. [What's that noise?] Oh, it's a couple of 'men 'arguing.
  c. [What's going on?] It's a 'woman 'crying.
  d. Listen. 'Listz is 'playing.

「出来事文」の強勢パターンから逸脱するケースがもう2つある。それは generic subjects（総称的主語）を伴う文や、ものごとの定義、特性、真理を

課題 45　　event sentence「出来事文」

伝える文も double stress になり、述語動詞に核強勢が来る。

a. ˈWood ˈfloats.
b. ˈPenguins ˈswim.
c. ˈBirds ˈsing.
d. Aˈwolf ˈhowls, ˈnot ˈbarks.
e. An ˈowl ˈhooted.
f. ˈHope ˈfaded.
g. ˈNature ˈcalls.（便意）
　　cf. A: Dad?
　　　　B: Yeah?
　　　　A: ˈStan ˈCrossman called.
　　　　B: OK. I'll call him back.

また、副詞が主語と述部の間に介入するときは、述部にも文強勢（核強勢）が来る。

l. The ˈcar *mysˈteriously* [1] broke down.
m. The ˈlight *ˈsuddenly* [1] went out.
n. ˈJohnson *unexˈpectedly* died.
o. ˈThis ˈtelegram [1] *just* came.

教室の音声学

課題 46　　文末の副詞（再訪）

　今日、コーパス（corpus）という用語が言語に関する話題によく出てくる。その意味は、a large collection of written or spoken language that is used for studying the language: *a corpus of spoken English*（言語資料）である。

　私が、本書で紹介する用例の大半は、映画中のセリフを聴きとったもので、作ったものではない。SUPRAS の "housekeeper" であった *Clear Speech*（Cambridge University Press）の著者 Judy Gilbert から以下のメールがあった。

> Your use of movies as a "corpus" is very interesting to me. I consider movies an important reflection of culture. Also, more recent movies have used more realistic language. So your project is quite original and should be very useful for serious students of English. (September 21, 2001)

1. once には、(i) on one occasion only（1回だけ）　(ii) at some time in the past, but not now（かつて）という意味があるが、前者は、意味的に重要であるので文強勢（しばしば核強勢）を受け、一方、後者は、意味的には minor (secondary) importance であるので文強勢を受けない。

   a. After that, a few weeks went by and I didn't see her ↘ *ONCE*.（一度も）
   b. My Dad and I went ↘ SKYdiving *once*.（かつて）

   文献からでは

   ・ ¹Mary was ¹here ¹once, but her husband used to come quite often.
   　once = numeral adverb
   ・ ¹Mary ¹used to ¹live here once; now she has gone to Paris.
   　once = indefinite adverb of time

   　　　Maria Schubiger, *The Role of Intonation in Spoken English* (1935:20)

2. then には (i) at that time　(ii) in that case という意味がある。

   a. Prices were not so high ↘ *THEN*.（その時）
   b. We'll see you on ↘ TUESday *then*.（それでは）

　しかし、once が「かつて」の意味をもつにもかかわらず、かなり目立って聞こえることがよくある。その場合、once が（低）上昇になっている（p.46参照）。実際には、文が2つの音調単位で発音されている。

   c. A: Why don't you settle down and get married, Walter?

課題 46　　文末の副詞（再訪）

　　　B: Why don't *you*, for instance?
　　　A: I almost ↘ DID | ↗ ONCE. A long time ago.
d.　I had a broken ↘ ARM | ↗ ONCE.
e.　A: I'm thinking of going to Costa Rica.
　　　B: Great! I ↘ WENT to Costa Rica | ↗ ONCE.
f.　A: Octopus and squid? How can you eat that stuff?
　　　B: You should try it. It's good for you.
　　　A: I ↘ DID have octopus | ↗ ONCE.

他の文末の副詞（句／節）も、意味的には二次的となり（低）上昇調になることがよくある。

(i)　I don't ↘ KNOW him actually.
(ii)　I don't ↘ KNOW him | ↗ ACtually.

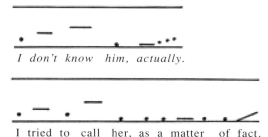

Laurie Bauer, et al, *American English Pronunciation* (1980:231)

(i)　I haven't ↘ SEEN him yet.
(ii)　I haven't ↘ SEEN him | ↗ YET.

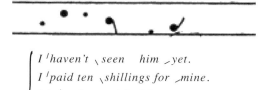

This is one of the most frequent patterns of English intonation. If there are several secondary stresses in the tail, the rise generally occurs in the last.

　　　Maria Schubiger, *English Intonation: Its Form and Function* (1858:19)

また、now や the other day, yesterday のような common adverbs of time を含む文でも両パターンがある。

```
  ─  \   _ ─ _              ─  \   _ ─ /
I saw George  the other day.   I saw George  the other day.

(So) you went to Malvern yesterday.   I went to Malvern yesterday.
  . . •  \  . . .              . . •  \  . . .
```

課題 47　　**polite correction** のイントネーション

以下の（1B）と（2B）の発言 Yes, I do. は、互いにイントネーションが異なる。

(1) A: Do you like it?
　　B: Yes, I do.
(2) A: You don't like that.
　　B: Yes, I do.　　（polite correction）

（1B）では↘ Yes, I ↘ do. となり、一方、（2B）では↘ Yes, | I ↗ do. と言う。それぞれの対話のイントネーションを詳しく表すと左図のようになる。

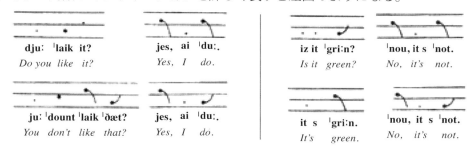

Daniel Jones, *English Phonetics* (9th Edition; 1960:312)

以下の（3B）と（4B）のイントネーションも互いに異なる。

(3) A: Is it green?
　　B: No, it's not.
(4) A: It's green.
　　B: No, it's not.　　（polite correction）

今回、このような種類のイントネーションを採りあげたのは、EP book 2, pp.38-39 に以下の内容があるからである。

No, I did not. は、激しい反駁の文である。準拠テープを聞いてみると↘No, I I did ↘not. と発音されている。つまり、(2B) と (4B) の上昇調のパターンとは矛盾しているが、絵を見ると納得できる。<u>男性が女性を責めて（非難して）いて、女性が毅然としてそれを撥ねつけている。</u>(He is pointing an <u>accusing finger</u> at her.) 率直に言って、このような下降調のイントネーションは、一般的な社交の場では用いられることが少ない。もっと polite な言い方は ↘No, I ↗didn't. である。以下で詳しく解説をしよう。

まず、(2B) と (4B) の下降調＋上昇調は polite correction のための contradiction intonation として知られている慣用パターンである。それに対して、下降調は、無礼な、ぶっきら棒な態度を表す。Wells, *English Intonation* (2006:31) に明解な解説がある。

> If we think someone has made a mistake, and we want to correct them, it is polite to do so in a tentative way. This explains the use of the fall-rise for polite corrections... In contrast, <u>to use a falling tone for a correction would be abrupt and perhaps rude</u>.　（斜線と太字は、筆者が追加）

また、毎年 8 月にロンドン大学（University College London）で開催される英語音声学講座（Summer Course）の常連の講師 Patricia Ashby も以下のように述べている。

　Polite vs. impolite (rude)

This is especially important to master when you are disagreeing with someone or contradicting them but you want to do this without giving offence. The fall-rise tune is usually used to this effect. Compare:

A: The news is on at nine

B: It's \not. ‖ It's at \ten. (rude)

　　　It's ∨not. ‖ It's at ∨ten. (polite)　　(from a handout in 2006)

相手から You're late. と言われて、↘No, I'm ↘not. は、いわば喧嘩腰の口調とも聞きとれる。Jack Windsor Lewis の解説が興味深い。激しく反論するときでさえも下降調＋上昇調のイントネーションで言われ、逆に、下降調は、友情に破綻をもたらすことを暗示するほど激しい怒りの響きがある。

> Even *fierce* contradictions are normally expressed by native English speakers with such a Rise (eg. *Oh,* ↘*no, I'm* ↗*not*.) because

課題 47　polite correction のイントネーション

it'd be crushing not to do so and it'd sound so angry as to suggest the complete end to a friendship! This is well worth noting because I've found it one of the very few choices of inappropriate pitch patterns that I've heard from EFL students I've asked to read such sentences aloud.

(PhonetiBlog, August 6, 2009)

課題 48　　　I know her. の特異なイントネーション

　中学校の英語教科書に準拠した音声資料を聴いていると、英語教師が戸惑うだろうと思われるイントネーションが随所にある。例えば、*New Horizon Book One*（旧版）には以下のような対話がある。

　A: Do you see that tall man? That's Hideki.
　　 Do you know him?
　B: Yes. He's a baseball player.
　A: Do you see that woman with
　　 short hair?
　B: Yes, <u>I know her</u>. That's Meg.

下線部は、通常ならば、動詞に核強勢を置いて I ↘know her. というイントネーションになる。ところが声優（子ども）は、↘I know ↗her. と発音している。前者と後者とでは、意味（shades of meaning）がどのように違うのだろうか。後者では、her が目立って発音されているからといって、him と対比されているわけでもない。I についても他の人物との対比ではない。実は、このようなイントネーションは、<u>突如、何かに気づき、それに興味を示す</u>ときに用いられる。このイントネーションは、論理的には説明ができないので intonation idiom と考えられる。確認のために SUPRAS のメンバーたちに発信すると、以下の返信があった。

　・Positively interested and ready to go on talking.
　・In this dialog, there is stress on ***her***, but not strong, contrastive stress, just more than ***know***. There is still stress on ***I*** also, but again not contrastive. So, the pitch starts out fairly high on ***I***, then drops for the softly spoken ***know***, then has a mild rise in ***her***.
　・It's one of the ways I'd say it, too. I use this intonation when I have <u>suddenly</u> succeeded in digging from my memory a face with a name and I'm now quite sure it's the one in the photo.

次も、表題の I know her. のイントネーションと同じパターンである。
　A: (Hanging up the phone) That was Susie Farkas.
　B: Susie Farkas? ↘I re<u>mem</u>ber ↗her. I had this big crush on her all the way
　　 through high school.　　注：crush 熱烈な恋心

既に課題 18 では、↘I ↗know. を紹介した。これも突然に何かを思いついたり、

課題 48　　I know her. の特異なイントネーション

納得したときの intonation idiom である。
　A: And who do you work for?
　B: I work for AJ dot com.
　A: Ah, ↘I ↗know. Do you sell computers?
　B: Yes, we do.

Wells からのコメントを再度紹介しよう。

<u>This is an intonation idiom</u>. When "I know" is used to say that you have suddenly had an idea or suddenly thought of a solution to a problem, it has two nuclear accents, fall plus rise. \I /know.

類似例を挙げると

a.　A: Peter's left us.
　　B: Left you? What happened to him?
　　A: He's got a new job in Edinburgh.
　　B: Oh, of course, yes. ↘I re↗member.

b.　A: You mean that when you give something that helps somebody else, you'll help yourself, too?
　　B: Exactly! Giving makes you strong.
　　A: Oh, ↘I ↗see.

更には、I ↘know ↗him. というパターンもよく聞かれる。

c.　A: John Cleese is a very funny actor.
　　B: ¹Oh \yes. | I've \seen /him.

Adapted from Peter Roach, *English Intonation and Phonology* (2000:177)

d.　I had a look into the wallet (忘れ物), and there was some money, and some cards and tickets and so on, and a photo. I looked at the photo and suddenly I thought: I ↘knew ↗him. It was an old friend from school.

e.　A: Hey, I ↘know ↗you.
　　B: Hi. Nice to meet you.

f.　A: Hi, Dad. This is Josh. He's a great baseball player.
　　B: (to Josh) Oh, yeah. I re↘member ↗you. You bat left and throw right.
　　　　　　　　　　　　　　　　　　　　　　（右投げ左打ち）

課題 49　　I thought it was going to rain.

　昔、日本英語音声学会関西中国支部研究大会で研究発表をした。Japanese Learners' L1 Transfer in English Word Focus という題であった。英語における日本人学習者の母語移入に関する発表であった。原稿のネタは、私がアメリカの TESOL 関係のニューズレター Speech/Pronunciation Interest Section Newsletter（SPRIS）で発表した論文である。
研究発表の後半で、私は次のように述べた。

　　Compared to English, Japanese is far less dependent on strong changes in pitch, loudness and length to convey differences in meaning; therefore, Japanese speakers are likely to be indifferent to those features. Instead, the Japanese language has a large repertoire of particles to serve the same purpose.

そして以下のような例を挙げた。
　(1) A: Are you sure he's a good teacher.
　　　B: ↘Yes, he ↘is a good teacher.　　　（本当に）
　(2) A: How come you were so quiet together?
　　　B: There was ˈnothing ↘to say.　　（言うことなんて）
　(3) A: I don't like fish and chips. I don't like burgers, either.
　　　B: ˈWhat ↘do you like?　　（一体、何が）
　(4) A: Thank you.
　　　B: ˈThank ↘you.　　（こちらこそ）
　(5) I ˈthought it was going to ↘rain.　　（...と思ったんだが）
　(6) I ↘thought it was going to ↗rain.　　（やっぱり...と思った）

期待、希望、危惧していたことが、実際に実現したか否かを伝える文も、以下に述べるように、大きくイントネーションに依存している。日本語なら、「やっぱり」「案の定」「生憎」「〜のに」を付けさえすれば、イントネーションに頼る必要がない。

　さて、自分の予想が当たるということは、予想した内容が場面に存在するので、既知情報としての扱いになり、上昇調で言われる。一方、自分の予想が外れるということは、発した情報内容が場面に存在していず、新しい情報として取り扱われることになり、下降調で言われる。以下の店頭での会話で、2 つの we can't help you. のイントネーションが、なぜ互いに異なるのかが分かるだろう。

課題 49　　I thought it was going to rain.

a.　A(*customer*): Do you sell garden tools, please?
　　B(shopkeeper): *I'm af'raid we 'can't ↘ help you, sir.*
　　A: Any idea where I should try?
　　B: What about Cook's in the Market Place?
　　A: That's an idea. I'll go down there now. Many thanks.
　　B: Well, *I'm ↘ sorry we 'can't ↗ help you.*

b.　Hi, Andrea. Nice to see you. I was ↘ hoping you could ↗ come. （予想的中）

c.　So, you can't come after all. What a pity! I was 'hoping you could ↘ come.
　　　　（予想外れ）

d.　I was af'raid it would ↘ snow.　（予想外れ：It did not snow.；下記の左図）
　　I was af ↘ raid | it would ↗ snow.　（予想的中：It snowed.；下記の右図）

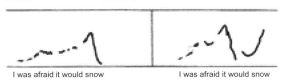

再度、以下の例で確認しよう。

e.　「やっぱり彼はそれをやれると思った」
　　　I ex ↘ pected he could ↗ do it.
　　「彼はそれをやれると思ったのに」
　　　I ex'pected he could ↘ do it.

f.　「やっぱり心配していたように電車が延着になった」
　　　We ↘ feared that the train would be ↗ late.
　　「電車が延着すると心配したが（そうでもなかった）」
　　　We 'feared that the train would be ↘ late.

また、短縮形の文 I ↘ thought you ↗ did. と I 'thought you ↘ did. にも以上の解説が適用できる。

Pattern (for an expected reply).　　*Pattern* (for an <u>un</u>expected reply).
A. *You* `knew him, | ╱didn't you? B. `Yes.　　A. *You* `knew him, | ╱didn't you? B. `No. or ╱No.

A. *I* `THOUGHT you ╱did.　　B. –*I* ╱thought you `DID.

W. Stannard Allen, *Living English Speech* (1954:149&152)

課題 50　　be 動詞の強勢

韻律上、be 動詞は機能語であるので、文中では弱勢になることが多い。しかし、文末や休止前では他の機能語である助動詞と前置詞と同様に強勢を受ける。

弱勢：He is busy.　He will come here.

強勢：ˈYes, he ↘is.

　　　ˈSo I ↘am.

　　　ˈYes, I ↘will.

　　　ˈWhere're you ↘from?

　　　ˈWho is it ↘by?

しかし、文末や休止前以外に位置しても be 動詞が強勢を受けることが多々ある。その場合、full verb である。

(1) 会合などに招待された際に、挨拶の冒頭に言われることばとして

　a.　It's ˈnice to ↘be here. /I'm ˈglad to ↘be here.

　その他、

　b.　He ˈcan't ↘be there tomorrow; he's busy.

　c.　ˈHow ˈlong are you going to ↘be here?

　d.　He is a ˈcharming ⁽¹⁾person to ↘be with.

　e.　ˈWhat do you ˈwant to ↘be in the future?

　f.　China? I've ˈnever ↘been there.

　g.　We ˈare what we ↘eat.

　h.　To ↗be or ↗not to be, ˈthat is the ↘question.

ただし、前後に重要な情報が来ると be が弱勢になることがある。

　i.　Look, we're going to be ˈhere for a ˈfew ↘days. Why don't we rent a car?

　j.　It's 10:30 now. I told them to meet here by 10:15. They're supˈposed to be ˈhere by ↘now.

(2) 確認や対比用法の場合、be 動詞が強勢を受ける。

　a.　A: He is a good student, isn't he?

　　　B: ˈYes, he ˈcertainly ↘is a good student.

　b.　A: Are you sure she is a good cook?

　　　B: ˈOh, she ↘is a good cook.

　c.　A: Are you coming or not coming?

課題 50　　be 動詞の強勢

B: I ↘am coming.

(3) 助動詞 should と共に用いられた場合、be 動詞が強勢を受ける場合と、受けない場合がある。
- He should ↘be here.　（should ⇒ obligation）
- He ↘should be here.　（should ⇒ expectation）

前者は、I'm expecting him, but he's late. という気持ちを表し、後者では、話者の態度が neutral であり、「（見えないが）ここにいるでしょう」と憶測を表す。ある時、大学で教えているアメリカ人講師に確認したことがある。彼によると、He ↘should be here. は、淡々とした態度であるのに対して、He should ↘be here. は、impatience, irritation, or anger の態度が表れているという。少し、誇張された発言のように思えるが、neutral な態度を表す強勢パターンではないことは確かだ。

そう言えば、I'll ↘be there. と I'll be ↘there. という 2 つの言い方がある。これらは大差がなく、ほぼ interchangeable であるが、there に強勢があるほうが more neutral statement であり、be に強勢があると、stronger determination を伝える。

a. A: Mom has told you to be home early today.
B: I'll ↘be there.
b. A: The meeting is very important to the future of the company.
B: I'll ↘be there.

(4) 文末や休止の直前に位置する場合でも、be 動詞が強勢を受ける場合と、受けない場合がある。

a. Do you ˈknow ⁽ˡ⁾what ↘this is?
b. Do you ˈknow ⁽ˡ⁾what it ↘is?
c. I want to make some phone calls to the office to ˈsee ⁽ˡ⁾what the ˈlatest ↘news is.
d. She knew she had problems with her English, but she ˈdidn't ˈknow ⁽ˡ⁾what the ˈproblems ↘were.

既に課題 13 でも述べたが、以下も be 動詞の emphatic usage である。

d) I ↘am sorry.
e) You ↘are clever with your fingers.
f) ˈWhere ↘are you going?

g) The ˈweather ↘ is hot today.

東京の GDM メンバー諸氏が月例研修会でも使用している Quirk 等の *A Comprehensive Grammar of the English Language*（Longman）には以下のような記述がある。

　If normally unstressed operators receive stress (especially nuclear stress), the effect is often to add <u>exclamatory emphasis to the whole sentence</u>.

　　　　That WILL be nice!

　　　　What ARE you doing?

　　　　We HAVE enjoyed ourselves!（p.1372）

なお、operators とは、助動詞や be 動詞を指す。

課題 51　　助動詞と代名詞の強勢（再訪）

(i) 助動詞 will, do, be 動詞は、内容語と違って、その語そのものに一定の情報があるわけではない。話者は、そのような機能語に強勢を置く「異常な」方法によって、"My feelings are involved." というシグナルを送る。これは emotional emphasis である。その際に留意しなければならないのは、強勢を受けた機能語の意味だけが強調されているのではなく、<u>文全体が強調されている</u>ということである。それ故に、感嘆文に言い換えができる。

> When, however, the intensity applies to the auxiliary group, the sentence can almost always be paraphrased by an <u>exclamative</u> sentence beginning "How...!" or "What...!"
> ・We DID have fun!　　　　　　What fun we had!
> ・That WOULD be a good idea!　What a good idea that would be!
> ・The weather IS hot today!　　How hot the weather is!
>
> 　　　　　　　　　　　Hirst, *Intonative Features* (1977:116)

他の例を挙げよう。

a. That WOULD be nice.　(⇒ That would be very nice!)
b. What ARE you doing?　(⇒ [in surprise] What on earth are you doing?)
c. We HAVE enjoyed ourselves.　(⇒ We've enjoyed ourselves very much.)
d. A: George, dear. Let me introduce you to our new neighbor.
   B: (to the neighbor) <u>How DO you do?</u>　(⇒ very cordial)
e. A: Would you like to do something tonight?
   B: Sure. I'd love to.
   A: What about an evening riverboat tour?
   B: Uh, actually I've gone twice this week.
   A: So, <u>what DO you want to do?</u> (⇒ insistent or impatient)
f. A: What's the matter?
   B: Nothing…nothing.
   A: <u>Something IS wrong.</u> What is it?　(⇒ I'm sure of that.)
g. A: Here's something for your sister.
   B: <u>Betty WILL be pleased.</u>　(⇒ She'll be very pleased!)

(ii) 代名詞

代名詞も機能語であるので原則的には強勢を受けないが、もし強勢を受けることがあれば、通例、他者との対比になる。しかし、時には対比される相手が必ずしも明らかでないことがある。その際、話者の態度は neutral ではなく、何らかの感情移入がある。例えば、発言に驚き、怒り、苛立ち、疑念などが表出されている。例えば、Who ARE you? (neutral) と Who are YOU? と比較すれば、後者の方には challenging な態度が入っている。

a. A: <u>Who are YOU?</u> What do you want?
    B: My name is Lockwood. I've lost my way on the moors.
    A: Strangers have no business on the moors at this time of year. Go away.

b. A: (引っ越してきて) Here we are.
    B: Phew! These bags are heavy.
    A: (noticing a woman inside) Excuse me, but <u>who are YOU?</u>
    C: Who am I? <u>Who are YOU?</u> This isn't your apartment. It's my apartment.
    A: This is our apartment.
    C: No, yours is next door!

c. <u>What are YOU doing up so early?</u> I thought you were on vacation this week.

d. Mr. Roberts! What a surprise! <u>What brings YOU here?</u> (注：いつも現在形)

e. A: Hey, <u>what happened to YOU?</u> You have a black eye. (目にあざ)
    B: I walked into the door. (ドアーにぶつかった)

f. Why, Shelby, <u>I wasn't expecting to see YOU here today.</u>

g. (じろじろ見つめる男に向って) <u>What are YOU looking at?</u>

h. <u>Who are YOU to give advice</u>, huh? <u>Who are YOU?</u>

i. A: Are you all right?
    B: <u>What do YOU care?</u> You never pay attention to me.

j. <u>What do *I* care about Tara?</u> I hate Tara!

k. <u>I'll never go out on a date with HIM!</u> (あんな奴)

l. He's a very difficult man. <u>We won't get much help from HIM.</u>

m. A: I'm very interested in Jesus Christ. [An awkward silence] Have I said anything wrong?
    B: No, but <u>we don't usually speak of HIM so casually.</u>　　(B は修道女)

n. A: Daddy, how do you spell *hallelujah*?
    B: <u>How should *I* know?</u> What do you think I am, a dictionary?

課題51　助動詞と代名詞の強勢（再訪）

なお、代名詞が核強勢ではなく強勢を受ける exclamatory questions がある。

a. Hello, darling! Did you miss me? Boy, did 'I miss YOU!
b. Oh, am 'I glad to see YOU! Come on in.
c. A: Do you like the present?
   B: Golly, do 'I LIKE it!
d. A: Have you seen the little Cathy recently?
   B: Yes. Boy, has 'she GROWN!

また、挨拶表現 How are you? が、冒頭から How are YOU? と発音されることがある。これも emotional emphasis で、親しみの感情が込められている。Bolinger には以下の文例がある。

・Good morning. How are YOU? (as an opener, not as a response)

Bolinger, *Intonation and Its Parts* (1986:78)

また、SUPRAS の会員が興味深いコメントを送ってきた。

At least among the General American speakers where I live, "How are YOU?" is the only pattern that sounds right as an opener. The pattern "How ARE you?" would only be used here as a repetition of the same opener when the respondent has been avoiding it and talking about something else:

A: How are YOU?
B: Well, I've had a lot to do today. My garden's doing well. They're repaving the street I live on.
A: Okay, but how ARE you?　（注：この場合、insistent）

"How are YOU?" ("you" is short) is an opener, not as a response.

"How are YOU?" ("you" is long) would be said when the person has responded to the opener by telling how other people are and not mentioning himself.　(2005.8.15)

次に、皮肉または反駁を表す慣用表現 You should talk! を紹介しよう。以下は、年配の男女間の対話である。

① A: Happy birthday, Lucinda.
   B: Thank you, my dear.
   A: You're remarkably well... for your age, that is.
   B: ↘↗ You should talk!　（実際の発音では ↘ You should talk ↗.）
   （⇒よく言うわね［貴方もいい年よ］）

② A: You know who you sound like when you talk? The mouse in *Tom and Jerry* cartoons?

　　B: Are you kidding me?

　　A: No, I figured it out.

　　B: ↘↗ You should talk! You have a whiny voice.

Wells は、blog でこの慣用表現のイントネーションについて

　　I think that's plain Fall-Rise, nucleus (tonic) on *you*, tail spread out so that the rise part comes on *talk*:

　　　∨ You should talk!

　　　∨ You're a fine one to talk!　　(2002. 3. 18)

　　　　(↘ 実際には ↘ You're a fine one to talk ♪)

しかし、私は下降調も聞いた。

③ A: What are you gonna do with the three steam irons?

　　B: Well, you never know when the two of them are gonna break down.

　　A: That's the most ridiculous thing I've heard of.

　　B: You know, ↘ you should talk! You bought a 100-pound sack of dog food.

　　A: Oh, that was half-price. (*The Lucy Show*)

自分の意見を述べる際の前置きの表現では、代名詞が強勢を受ける。

① Some people say that science clears up all the mysteries for us. In ↘↗ my opinion, it only creates more.

② A: No smoking in public places? But this is my office!

　　B: Offices are considered public places, as ˈfar as ↘↗ I'm concerned.

③ If you ˈask ↘↗ me, you treat women as if they were your maids.

④ To Sherlock Holmes, she is always the best woman. In ↘↗ his eyes, she represents the very best of all women.

自宅を表す意味の my place, our place では、代名詞が強勢を受ける。

① ˈLet's go to ˈmy place and ˈplay games.

② We're ˈhaving a ˈparty at our place next week.

最後に、形容詞に後続する代名詞 one の強勢について述べたい。

えっ！そんなことがあるのかと驚く人がいるだろう。通例、

　　I have a dog; it's a ˈmixed-pedigree *one*.

課題 51　　助動詞と代名詞の強勢（再訪）

　　　Would you like a <u>green</u> *one* or a <u>red</u> *one*?
となり、one は強勢を受けない。
では、the wrong one ではどうだろうか。実は、one は強勢を受ける。
　　　You've ˈgiven me the ˈwrong <u>one</u>.
John Maidment（元ロンドン大学教員）は、blog で次のように述べている。
　　　For many years I have thought this decidedly odd. The word *one* (similarly *ones*) certainly cannot be deemed new information, and the adjective, whatever it is, certainly *is* new information. After probably 30 years, I am still waiting for a eureka moment.　　(September 23, 2009)
また、the one, the right one, the only one, the first/last one, which one でも、one が強勢（しばしば核強勢）を受ける。これらも説明ができない idiomatic intonation である。

課題 52　　Thank you VERy (SO) much.

　Thank you very MUCH. は中立的強勢パターンであるが、Thank you VERy (SO) much. という発音もある。感謝の表現だけにとどまらない。同情や遺憾の気持ちを、より効果的に表わすために、I'm SO sorry. と発音することもある。一般的には、副詞＋副詞や副詞＋形容詞では、被修飾語のほうが major stress を受けるが、逆転現象が起こり、修飾語のほうが強調されることがある。Leech & Svartvik は以下の解説をしている。

　　The words "so" and "such" are stressed and, for extra emphasis, may receive nuclear stress.

　　　　　　　A *Communicative Grammar of English* (1994:153)

a. 映画『逢引き』（鉄道の駅のホームで）

　　A: [B（女性）の目に埃（grit）が入ったのを目撃し] Can I help?

　　B: Oh, no, please. It's only something in my eye.

　　A: Please let me look. I happen to be a doctor.

　　B: <u>It's VERy kind of you.</u>

　　A: [after a moment] There!

　　B: [blinking] Oh, what a relief — it was agonizing.

　　A: It looks like a bit of grit.

　　B: <u>Thank you VERy much.</u>

感謝や謝罪の表現だけではなく、修飾語が major stress（しばしば核強勢）受けるケースを挙げておこう。

b. <u>VERy well, then.</u> Let's complete the paperwork.

c. <u>I'm VERy glad</u> you and the Smiths have met.

d. A: So you enjoyed the visit to the Motor Show last Saturday, John?

　　B: Yes, <u>VERy much indeed</u>, Peter.

e. She knows a lot about horses, and she rides VERy well.

f. I was pleased to hear of your coming marriage. <u>Your father must be VERy happy.</u>

g. [over the PA system] On behalf of the captain and crew, I'd like to welcome you to Los Angeles. <u>Have a VERy merry Christmas.</u>

h. <u>It's been SUCH a lovely evening</u>, my dear. Pleasant company, too.

課題 52　　Thank you VERy (SO) much.

i.　A: At home, in Australia, we open our presents as soon as they come. Sometimes there's nothing left to open on Christmas Day.

　　B: That sounds VERy dull.

j.　A: Are you suggesting that I forget the whole affair?

　　B: Exactly. For your own sake as well as ours.

　　A: VERy well.

k.　A: Mother, whatever happened to all our money, anyway?

　　B: Jack, I told you SO many times. It was stolen from us.

Maria Schubiger の解説を見よう。

> Shifted stress
>
> The strongest stress, and therefore the nuclear glide, occurs on a word which in less emotional speech would be pre-nuclear, often even unstressed.
>
> *English Intonation: Its Forms and Functions* (1958:107)

彼女からの例を挙げておこう。

・She's a VERy nice woman.

・They're MUCH better, thank you.

・I QUITE agree.

・She's a MOST charming person.

・That'll be a GREAT help.

・He's SO droll.

・That's a PLEASant touch of colour.

Daniel Jones は、We're SO sorry. という強勢パターンについて、以下のように述べている。不可解であると言っている。

> The intonation described... is sometimes used in situations where there does not appear to be any obvious contrast and where it is therefore difficult to specify the reason for the use of the intonation.
>
> *English Phonetics* (1960:305)

課題 53　　　イントネーションが意味を区別する

イントネーションには様々な機能があるが、以下が主な機能である。
a. 話者の感情や態度を表す。
b. 音調単位中の最も重要な語を明示する。
c. 句、節、文の間の境界を示したり、文の種類を明示する。
d. 音調単位中の新情報と既知情報とを区別する。
但し、複数の機能が同時に絡むことがある。
さて、これから、表層構造では同じ表現が、イントネーションによって違った意味をもつケースを考察してみよう。

a. I walked and jogged a lot every day. Good-bye, sugar. No more sugar. Now I'm slim.
　① ˈGood ⁽ˡ⁾bye, ↘sugar.（断糖宣言）
　② ˈGood ↘bye, | ↗sugar.（恋人との別れ）

b. *Can you spare me a few minutes?*
　① Can you ˈspare me a ˈfew ↗minutes?
　　　(= Can you give me a few minutes of your time?)
　② Can you ↗spare me (for) a few minutes?
　　　(= Will you excuse my absence for a few minutes?)

c. *He didn't die happily.*
　① He ˈdidn't ˈdie ↘happily.
　　　(= He didn't die a happy death; he died miserably.)
　② He ˈdidn't ↘die | ↗happily (= fortunately)
　　　(= It was fortunate that he didn't die)

d. *He drives normally.*
　① He ˈdrives ↘normally. (= in a normal manner)
　② He ↘drives, | ↘↗normally. (= He usually drives; he's in the habit of driving)

なお、sentence-final adverbials は、しばしば低上昇調になる。

e. *My sister who lives in Edinburgh has just had twins.*
　① My ↘↗sister, | who ˈlives in ↘↗Edinburgh, | has ˈjust ⁽ˡ⁾had ↘twins.
　　　(= my only sister, who happens to live in Edinburgh)
　② My ˈsister who ˈlives in ↘↗Edinburgh | has ˈjust had ↘twins.

課題 53　イントネーションが意味を区別する

(= I have sisters, and the one who lives in Edinburgh has just had twins.)

f. *He doesn't drink because he is ill.*
   ① He ˈdoesn't ↘drink, | because he is ↘ill.
   否定の範囲は drink までしか及ばない。従って、主文と従属文は独立した音調単位を構成する
   ② He ˈdoesn't ˈdrink because he is ↘↗ill.
   （病気だから飲酒しないのではない〔他の理由がある〕）
   否定の範囲は主文と従属文の全体に及び、1 tone unit を構成する。

g. *She didn't come because of bad weather.*
   ① She ˈdidn't ˈcome because of ˈbad ↘weather.
   ② She ˈdidn't ˈcome because of ˈbad ↘↗weather.
   （悪天候のせいで来なかったのではない）

h. *She doesn't date any man.*
   ① She ˈdoesn't ⁽ˡ⁾date any ↘man.
   ② She ˈdoesn't ⁽ˡ⁾date ↘↗any man. （どんな男性ともデートするわけではない）

i. *I don't lend my car to anybody.*
   ① I ˈdon't ⁽ˡ⁾ lend my ˈcar to ↘anybody.
   ② I ˈdon't ⁽ˡ⁾ lend my ˈcar to ↘↗anybody. （誰にでも車を貸すのではない）

j. *I wasn't listening all the time.*
   ① I ˈwasn't ˈlistening ˈall the ↘time.
   ② I ˈwasn't ˈlistening ↘all the ↗time. （ずっと聞いていたのではない）

k. ① Soldier: We've got an order, ma'am. Nobody's leaving here without being searched.
   　　Cathy: Go ahead. ↘Search me.
   ② A: Why did they break up?
   　B: Who?
   　A: Simon and Garfunkle.
   　B: ˈSearch ↘↗me. (I don't know)

l. ① A: Why didn't Phil come to the meeting yesterday?
   　B: He ↘said | he was ˈtoo ↘busy. (I doubt it.)
   ② A: Why didn't Phil come to the meeting yesterday?
   　B: He ˈsaid he was ˈtoo ↘busy. (ordinary type)

課題 54　　No, it isn't. vs. No, it is not.

まず、率直な気持ちとして、Is this yours? に対して、is を強調して No, it ISn't. と発音するのは理屈に合わない。肯定か否定かが話題になっているときに、意味を決定づける否定語の not ではなく、繰り返しの語 is が最も強調されている。一方、No, it is NOT. は理に叶っている。「～であるか（is...）と問われて、「～ではありません（is not）」は、すっきりしている。では、なぜ意味的に重要な否定語 not が " 軽んじられ "、接尾語のように be 動詞に付加されているのか。

まず、考えられることは、音調単位の冒頭が、No で始まると、それがいわば露払い役になり、主文は negation になることが明らかである。日本語では「お疲れではありませんか」と尋ねられて「はい、疲れていません」というのか可能であるが、英語では Yes, I'm not tired. とは言えない。No, I'm not tired. でしかありえない。冒頭の No に続くのは「否定文」でなければならない。あるネイティブ・スピーカーの友人によれば、Once *No* has been said, the negation is in play; it is contextually clear.

次に、Is this yours? に対して、No, it is not. という full form（option b）も考えられるが、短縮形 No, it isn't. とはどのような意味的違いがあるのだろうか。前者の full form は厳しい反駁の語調になる。何しろ No と発したら、文を否定する概念が文脈上明らか ── the negation is in play ── であるにもかかわらず、再度、否定を表す語 not を使うのは、怒りや反目などの態度を伝えている。当然のことながら、顔の表情も厳しくなるだろう。海外の研究者と意見交換する中で、1 人は、次のように言う。

> Option b would be re-selecting the negation when both speaker and hearer know it is in the air, and in many contexts, perhaps, this would be regarded as rude or face-threatening.

私が、これまで何度も教示を乞うてきた Jack Windsor Lewis は、普通の会話では "he is not" という full form は避けるべきであると言う。なぜならば、それは苛立ちや怒りを表わすからである（p.153 参照）。

> It never occurs in present-day ordinary un-emphatic purely conversational usage. The pronunciation such a phrase suggests, when it occurs in less ordinary styles, is more deliberate than just a normally emphatic version.

課題 54   No, it isn't. vs. No, it is not

It's thus best avoided altogether by the EFL learner because it may suggest *impatience*, *exasperation* or the like.

例えば、

　A: You must be joking.
　B: ↘ No, | I am ↘ not. (impatience, exasperation, etc.)

a. ［2 人の仲良し子どもの会話で、1 人がもう帰ると言い出すと、相手は不機嫌になる］

　　A: I have to go home and take a nap.
　　B: ˈDo ↘ not.
　　A: ↘ *Do,* | ↗ *too*.
　　B: ˈDo ↘ not.
　　A: ↘ *Do,* | ↗ *too*.

この場合の、末尾の too は特殊な意味で、大部分の日本人には馴染みのない用法である。これは、「ところが、実際には」の意味である。

b. 　A: You're not smart enough to use a computer.
　　B: I ↘ *am,* | ↗ *too*.

c. 　A: I don't go there often.
　　B: You ↘ *do,* | ↗ *too*.

d. 　A: Bad girl! If Santa finds out, he won't bring you any toys.
　　B: There is no Santa Claus.
　　A: There ↘ *is,* | ↗ *too*. I saw him.
　　B: You mean that man dressed like Santa Claus in the department store. He's a fake.

e. 　A: Every girl thinks of getting married to the man she loves.
　　B: I don't.
　　A: You will, my Jo. Someday.
　　B: ˈWill ↘ *not*.　(impatience, exasperation)

しかし、polite correction の場合、↘ *No,* | I ↗ *won't*. となる。

課題 55　　再帰代名詞の文強勢の有無

まず、以下の help(ed) himself には強勢パターンの違いがある。
 (i) When the roast came by, he ˈhelped him ↘self.
これは、served himself と同義であり、「（自ら給仕して）食べた」。
 (ii) He tried not to weep, but ˈcouldn't ↘help himself.
これは、couldn't control himself と同義であり、「こらえる（我慢する）ことができなかった」という意味である。また、文脈によっては、「仕方がなかった」という意味にもなる。さて、help oneself の意味の違いは、再帰代名詞が文強勢を受けるか否かにかかっている。(i) の場合は、文強勢があり、(ii) の場合は、文強勢がない。

　一般に、再帰代名詞が動詞の<u>目的語</u>として用いられる場合は、動詞のほうが強い強勢を受ける。従って、(i) は、例外的な強勢配置である。

 a. William, be ↘have yourself!
 b. You for↘get yourself, Father. I am no longer a child.
 c. We en↘joyed ourselves at the party.
 d. I ˈusually ↘shave myself / before ˈgoing to ↘bed.
 e. She ↘dressed herself.
 f. As he ran, he ↘timed himself.

次は、再帰代名詞における強勢の有無が、文の意味を区別する例である。

 g. ① He ↘asked himself.　［彼は自問した —himself は目的語］
    ② He ˈasked him ↘self.
       ［彼自身が質問した —himself は強調用法 (= He himself asked.]

 h. ① I've ˈnever ↘taught myself.　［独学の経験がない —myself は目的語］
    ② I've ˈnever ˈtaught my ↘self.
       ［私自身人を教えた経験がない —myself は強調用法］

 i. ① He ↘felt himself. (e.g., to see if he was injured)
       ［身体を触った —himself は目的語］
    ② He ˈfelt him ↘self. (i.e., he felt much more like his usual self)
       （普段の体調に戻った）

② は慣用表現で idiomatic intonation をもつ。I'm ˈnot ⁽¹⁾feeling my ↘self.
と言えば、I'm ˈnot ↘feeling well. という意味である。蛇足になるが、He's

174

課題 55　再帰代名詞の文強勢の有無

not himself. (= Something is wrong with him.); She was herself again. (= She was back to her usual self.)

また、再帰代名詞は、前置詞の目的語となる場合も、文強勢を受けない。

- j. I'm a ↘shamed of myself.
- k. He's ↘proud of himself.
- l. She ↘smiled to herself as if quite ↘satisfied.
- m. He beˈgan to ↘doze | in ↘spite of himself.（思わず）
- n. I was beˈside myself with ↘worry then.（我を忘れた）
- o. He ˈoften ↘talks to himself.
- p. Stand tall, boy. ˈHave some res↘pect for yourself.（自分に誇りをもて）
- q. Long time so see, Jack. ˈWhat have you been ↘doing with yourself?
- r. Well, ˈwhat do you ˈhave to ↘say for yourself?（どんな言い分があるか）

ただし、以下のような慣用表現では、再帰代名詞に文強勢（しばしば核強勢）がある。

- s. A: Shouldn't you cut down on drinking?

  B: ˈSpeak for your ↘self. You, too.（他人事みたいに言うなよ、君も同じだよ）
- t. We ˈhad the ˈbeach all to our ↘selves.（ビーチを独り占め）
- u. She ˈwent there ˈall by her ↘self.
- v. A: What would you like to eat for dinner?

  B: I'm not hungry.

  A: OK. ˈSuit your ↘self.
- w. A: Which one of the hats should I buy?

  B: ˈPlease your ↘self.（勝手にどうぞ）

教室の音声学

課題 56　　単語中に起こる強勢移動

　英語では、強勢のない音節が対比のために強勢を受けることがある。よく知られているのは、ˈlikes and ˈdislikes, ˈtrust and ˈmistrust, ˈhonest and ˈdishonest, ˈknown and ˈunknown などにおける接頭辞の強勢である。接尾辞も対比的に強勢を受けることがある。音調単位の中では、接尾辞が文強勢（しばしば核強勢）を受ける。

a. He's ˈnot ↘↗ tall, but tall ↘ er than us. (*tallER*)
b. I ˈcan't ˈsay it's ↘↗ cheap, but it's cheap ↘ ish. (*cheapISH*)
c. It ˈwasn't eˈxactly ↘↗ green, but it was green ↘ ish. (*greenISH*)
d. A: Are you ready?
　　B: ↘ Ish. (= more or less)

e. They're employ ↘ ers and employ ↘ ees.
f. We learned about ˈIndia and Indi ↘ ans.

ちょっと珍しいケースがある。sit-com を観ていたときに気づいた。

g. A: Stop making me feel so guilty, okay?
　　B: Brandon, let me just clarify something for you. I'm the one whose feelings were hurt.
　　A: So ˈI'm the hurt ↘ er and ˈyou're the hurt ↘ ee, | is ˈthat ↗ it?

但し、接尾辞は、通例は、弱音節である。

h. A: How old is he?
　　B: He's thirtyish.
i. ˈLet's ˈmeet at sixish.
j. He's Michael Jacksonish.（マイケル・ジャクソンっぽい）
k. It's a yellowish color.

ちょっと面白いのは boring である。通常は、第 1 音節に強勢があり、ˈboring であるが、第 2 音節にも強勢を置かれている事例をしばしば聞く。

ˈbo ↘ ˈring [ˈbɔː ˈrɪŋ]

176

課題 56　　単語中に起こる強勢移動

と少し長めに発音される。Wells の *English Intonation* (2006:187) にも言及がある。以下は、Cambridge University Press から出ている *Tactics for Listening* シリーズからの例である。

a. Peter's party was terrible. We had to play all sorts of stupid games. Then we watched a home video of his vacation in Hawaii.　例：ˈBo ↘ ring!

b. A few months ago I moved to this cute little house out in the country. Before I moved, all I did was sit in coffee shops and read or surf the Internet. ˈBo ↘ ring! Now I want to spend all my free time outside, enjoying nature...

c. A: The story is about a cat that can talk. It makes us laugh a lot and...

　　（中略）

B: Mark, there is nothing new about talking animals. The story is stupid. ˈBo ↘ ring!

また、sorry も double stress で言われることがある。昔、SUPRAS に向けて以下のような posting を発信した。それに対する返信が興味深い。この sorry は謝罪とは全く真逆の態度の表明である。皮肉や相手の理不尽な考えを軽べつしている。

　Dear all,

Would native speakers ever accent the second syllable of 'sorry' under some pragmatic circumstances (perhaps ironically)? I seem to have heard it recently in one of the episodes of the old Amerian sit-com *Growing Pains* (video version).

[In the living room, a tit for tat between teen-aged siblings]

　Brother: Dad, what's another word for 'election'?

　Sister:　'Plebiscite'.

　Brother: I didn't ask you. I asked Dad.

　Sister:　What's the difference?

　Brother: The difference is, I don't want to know from you.

　Sister:　ˈ*Sor* ↘ *ry.*

　Bother:　How do you spell it?

　Sister:　Why should I have to tell you how to spell it?

　Brother: Because I asked you.

Sister: I thought you didn't want to know from me.
Brother: What are you, a lawyer?

返信の一部を紹介しよう。

- My younger daughter does this all the time. *Iron*ic is not usually the interpretation I give it. It is her way of saying, "You're being unreasonable. I know you think I did something wrong, but I really didn't. I'll say I'm sorry, but I don't believe it for a second."
- Both my son and daughter used to do the same thing (they're now 25 and 21 and no longer do it). I used to put the same interpretation on it as John does for his daughter.

最近は *please* が double syllable で言われるのを聞くことがある。これは、相手の愚かな発言や不条理な発言対する "Don't be silly." や "Give me a break." の意味である ˈPuh-ˈlease." とか、ˈOh, ˈpuh-ˈlease! と言われる。

Mother: Do you want to try this broccoli?
Son: Oh, puh-lease. I had spinach for breakfast.（勘弁してよ）

課題 57　　名目上の **subject + predicate** のイントネーション

<small>This is the icebox.
Mary keeps the milk in the icebox.
She keeps it in the cold air.
The air in the icebox is cold.
The cold air keeps the milk cold.</small>

下記の第5文型の文の強勢配置は、次のようになる。

The ˈcold ↘↗ air ǀ ˈkeeps the ⁽¹⁾milk ↘ cold.

ここで目的語（milk）と目的補語（cold）は、名目上では subject + predicate の関係にある。

Cf. The milk is cold.

では、The icebox keeps food cold. でも、cold. が核強勢を受けるだろうか。実は、この文は、上記の The cold air keeps the milk cold. の場合のように、核強勢が文末の内容語に来ない。なぜなら food が初出の名詞だからである。これまで度々述べたように、初出の名詞は、音調単位の中で優先的に核強勢を受ける。従って、以下が妥当なイントネーションになる。

The ↘↗ icebox ǀ ǀ ˈkeeps ↘ food cold.

以下も、第5文型の文である。やはり目的語（名目上の主語）が核強勢を受け、目的補語（名目上の述部）は強勢を抑制され、尾部になる。

a. The koˈtatsu ⁽¹⁾keeps your ↘ legs warm.
b. I ˈcan't ⁽¹⁾keep my ↘ eyes open. I'm so sleepy.
c. She ˈtries to ˈkeep her ↘ figure slim; she works out at the gym.
d. She's a talkative person. She ˈcan't ⁽¹⁾keep her ↘ mouth shut.
e. I'm wearing sunglasses, because I ˈlike to ˈkeep my ↘ eyes dark.
f. It's really cold outside. ˈDon't ⁽¹⁾leave the ↘ door open.
g. She ˈwears her ↘ hair long.
h. Honey, open the door. I've ˈgot my ↘ hands full.
i. I'll ˈkeep my ↘ fingers crossed for you.　　（君の幸運を祈って）
j. I'm going to ˈhave my ↘ hair cut.
k. The ˈfood ⁽¹⁾makes my ↘ mouth water.

なお、核強勢の直後の形容詞と分詞は、核強勢の下降調の終結部を引き継ぐ尾部に過ぎず、独自のピッチ変化をもたないので比較的低く発音される。

次に付帯状況を表す前置詞句の場合も、名目上の subject + predicate の関係が見られる。

Do this ǀ with your ↘ eyes shut.

Cf. Your eyes are shut.

かつて、中学校の教科書 *New Horizon* 2 に以下のような passage があった。

> It was very cold, and it rained a lot that night. <u>Susan came home</u> | about ten o'clock. She was cold and tired. She opened the door and went into her room. <u>The windows were open</u>! Slowly the door next to the room opened. <u>A dark figure came in.</u> It came up to her | with <u>a knife in its hand</u>.

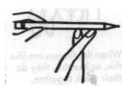

（下線と棒線は、伊達が付記）

最後の文中の付帯状況を表す前置詞句でも、a knife と in its hand は、subject + predicate の関係になり、初出名詞 knife が核強勢を受け、「場所の副詞」in its hand は尾部になる。

> It came up to her | with a ↘<u>knife</u> in its hand.

同様にして

a. He was waiting for me | with a ˈworried ↘<u>look</u> on his face.
b. He was born | with a ˈsilver ↘<u>spoon</u> in his mouth. （裕福な家に生まれた）
c. He came up to me | with a ↘<u>chip</u> on his shoulder. （けんか腰で）
d. He left home | with the ↘<u>lights</u> on.
e. I'm going out of my mind | with ˈall those ↘<u>bells</u> ringing. （気が変になりそう）
f. I made a speech in front of many people | with my ↘<u>heart</u> beating.
g. He quit the company | with his ↘<u>work</u> unfinished.
h. She walked up to me | with a ˈnice ↘<u>smile</u> on her face.

以上のように、英語では初出の名詞の「存在感」は特に注目に値するが、一方、日本人学習者は述部を強調する傾向が強い。上記の *New Horizon* 2 からの引用には、以下の文がある。

> Susan came home...
> The windows were open.
> A dark figure came in.

これらの文では、どのようなイントネーションになるか。特にどこに核強勢が来るか。恐らく大半の人が、次のように言うだろう。

> ˈSusan ˈcame ↘<u>home</u>...
> The ˈwindows were ↘<u>open</u>.

課題 57 　　名目上の subject + predicate のイントネーション

　　　　A ˈdark ˈfigure ˈcame ↘in.
しかし、それは妥当ではない。以下は、私が CD の声優の朗読を聴いて、記したものである。
　　　　↘Susan came home…
　　　　The ↘windows were open.
　　　　A ˈdark ↘figure came in.
なぜこのようなイントネーション ── 強勢配置 ── になるのか。これらは、event sentence（出来事文）である。「状態の変化」（change of state）、特に、出現、不慮の出来事、不運、失踪の内容を伝える。初出の名詞主語が核強勢を受け、動詞の強勢は抑制される。つまり、名詞主語が主情報、動詞は副次情報となる。

教室の音声学

課題 58　　**Here you are.** のイントネーション

　中学検定教科書や EP には Here you are. という構文がよく出てくる。どの語を最も強調して発音するのか、迷う人がいるだろう。即ち、核強勢は here に来るのか、それとも are に来るのか。このような構文では、here に主音調（fall）がある。

　　　Shop assistant: That will be eleven dollars for the two shirts, sir.
　　　Customer:　　　Here you are.

Hére you are.

Where are your scissors?
Here they are.

　また、There they are. も同じイントネーションになる。しかし、be 動詞に二次的な重要度を加えたい時には、上昇調で言う。実は、日常会話では Here you are. There you are. は、下降＋上昇調になるほうが多い。そこには、politeness も加味されていると考えることもできる。

　　　↘ Here you ↗ are.　　　　　　↘ There you ↗ are.

There you are. 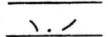 intonation used on pointing out or handing something.

Schubiger, *The Role of Intonation in Spoken English* (1935:72)

しかし、be 動詞の直後に休止（pause）がない場合には、それは弱形になる。

a.　A: Oh, ↘ there you are, Peter.
　　B: I'm sorry I couldn't get here earlier, John.

EP からの例では

b.　↘ Here they are in the ↘ earth.
　　Cf. ↘ Here she ↗ is, | ˈcoming into the ↘ ˈroom.

We get potatoes from the roots of a plant.

Here they are in the earth.

以前にも言ったように、EP の音声資料は 3 種類ある。ハーバード大学の Richards 作成の LP レコードと、洋販と IBC の CD である。これらを聴くと Here I am. は、共通して、下降調＋上昇調になっている。

　　　↘ Here I ↗ am.

課題 58　　Here you are. のイントネーション

c. Where's my book? Oh ↘ here it ↗ is.
d. I can't find my keys. Oh ↘ there they ↗ are! On the table.
e. A: ↘ Here we ↗ are.
   B: So this is your house.
   　Cf. ↘ Here we are, ↗ sir.

Here is Mary. She is coming into the room. She say, "Here I am"

なお、There you are. には「ほら、私の言ったとおりだろう」（What did I tell you?）の意味もある。以下は、その例である。

"You've got a capital view here, James." "*There you are!*" muttered James. "Why didn't you come before?"

Schubiger (1935:44)

また、There you go. も Here(There) you are. と同じ意味である。下降調もあるが、下降＋上昇調のほうが more friendly, courteous, or encouraging である。

A: Excuse me. Will you take my picture with this camera?
B: Sure, I'll be glad to. Ready? Smile. (Click!) ↘ There you ↗ go.

課題 59　　The books are here. vs. We have some books here.

今回のテーマは、here と there における文強勢の有無に関するものである。上記の例の normal stress pattern は、次のようになる。

　　The ˈbooks are ↘here.

　　We ˈhave some ↘books here.

では、文末にある here に文強勢（この場合、核強勢）を置いたり、置かなかったりする規則は何であろうか。

(1) いくつかの特定の動詞は、必ず補語（complement）として「場所の付加語」（adjunct of place）を要求する。例えば、put, send である。文意を伝えるのに場所の付加語を伴う。Put the books. は、ナンセンスである。一方、Put the books here. とか Put the books down. は妥当である。つまり、here と down は essential complements であるので、文強勢（核強勢）を受ける。右上図では、

　　ˈThis ˈtable is ↘here.　　ˈThat table is ↘there.

(2) We have some books here. 中の here は、circumstantial information を提供するだけであって、省略しても文意は通る。従って、文強勢を置かないのが通例である。右図では

　　　　It is ˈon a ↘hook there. You will ↘see it there.

とは言え、essential complements である here, there が既知情報（文脈に導入済みの項目）であるならば、文強勢を受けない。例えば、

"It is on a hook there. You will see it there."

She is putting it on the table.

She put it there.

　　She ↘put it there.

課題 59　　The books are here. vs. We have some books here.

　確かに、Richards の音声（LP レコード版）では put に核強勢を置いている、一方、洋販と IBC 版の CD では、She ˈput it ↘there. と言っている。英語の強勢配置規則の整合性を考えると、やはり、前者のほうに軍配が上がる。

　ただし、circumstantial information である here, there にもう少し重要度（二次的重要度：secondary importance）を与えたければ、上昇調で言うのが一般的である。つまり、here, there は上昇調の核強勢を受ける。文全体としては二つの音調単位に分かれ、下降調＋上昇調という複合音調になる。

　　We ˈhave some ↘books | ↗here.
　　You will ↘see it | ↗here.

そう言えば、中学校検定教科書準拠の CD でも、このような複合音調が聞かれる。

a. ① Brr... it's ↘cold in here.
   ② Brr... it's ↘cold | in ↗here.

b. A: Do you like living in Osaka?
   B: ① Yes. I ↘like it here.
   　　② Yes. I ↘like it | ↗here.

c. A: So how was the trip to Paris?
   B: ① ˈOh, I ↘loved it there.
   　　② ˈOh, I ↘loved it | ↗there.

d. A: Sorry to be late, Frank.
   B: You know, it's pretty cold, waiting here.
   A: Why didn't you wait in the waiting room? You would have been ˈmuch ↘warmer | ↗there.

課題60　　呼びかけ、警告、または、叱責のイントネーション

(1) calling

まず、少し離れたところにいる人を呼ぶときには、平坦調がよく用いられる。つまり、末尾で声が最後まで下がり切らずに、中途半端な平板調になる。→Bob→by となる。

・This type of intonation is used when calling to someone, usually at some distance away. A mother calling her child outdoors would use this intonation.

English Language Service, *Stress and Intonation*, Part 1 (1967:81)

Bóbbȳ.
Álān.

・The intonation pattern for calling someone is 2-3*-2. (p.11 の図を参照)
This pattern is similar to that of non-finality in that the final tone is a non-terminal fall. However, one important difference is that the final syllable of the intonational phrase is lengthened more than usual. An example of this would be a parent calling her child in from outside for dinner.

ELIZabeeeth. Time for DINNerrrrr.

Marianne Celce-Murcia et al. *Teaching Pronunciation* (2010:244)

(2) cautioning or reprimanding

警告したり、叱責するときは、中平坦調＋高平坦調が用いられる。

・You will hear this intonation when someone is cautioning or reprimanding. If a child is doing something he shouldn't, or is about to do something, you will hear the parent say his name in the following manner.

Stress and Intonation (p. 81)

Jóhnnȳ.
Bóbbȳ.
Álān.
Béttȳ.

課題 60　　呼びかけ、警告、または、叱責のイントネーション

このイントネーションは必ずしも子どもを叱責するときとは限らない。私自身も少しふざけすぎて不穏当なこと言った時に Mr. ⇗Da⇘te! と"叱られた"ことがある。また、叱責以外にも、子どもが母や父に抗議するときも

　　Oh, ⇗Mo⇘m!　　　Oh, ⇗Da⇘d! Give me a break!

映画からの例を挙げよう。

a. ある若い男性の噂をしていて

　Girl:　　　　I love his eyes.
　Grandma:　　I like his tight butt.（引き締まった尻）
　Girl:　　　　⇗Grand⇘ma!

b. 万引きの疑念

　Maki:　Yumi, that's an expensive ring! We don't have that much money. Where did you get it?
　Yumi:　None of your business. Forget it.
　Maki:　⇗Yu⇘mi!

c. Sharon:　Kevin, you need some modern clothes. You always wear the same things.
　Kevin:　I like these clothes.
　Sharon:　Well, I don't. They sell men's clothes upstairs. Come on.
　Kevin:　⇗Sha⇘ron!

d. レストランで食事中、料理について

　Woman:　What's wrong with them?
　Man:　They're the wrong shape and they're just awful.
　Woman:　Now, ⇗Ro⇘nald!
　Man:　The eggs look like you just laid them.
　Woman:　↘Ronald!（the form for a strong reaction,　reprimanding Ronald）

　　参考：↘Ronald! の例にあるように、真剣になって叱るときは下降調のほうが more powerful である。

　Mother:　Josh, I told you to take out the garbage.
　Son:　One minute.
　Mother:　Josh, didn't you hear what your mother said?
　Son:　One minute.
　Mother:　ˈJoshua ↘Baskin!
　Son:　OK, OK, OK.

以上の stylized intonation について Ladd (1978:184) は "a stepping-up sequence of level pitches" と称し、"It seems to be restricted to calls and parental admonitions ... and has a fairly fixed pitch interval of about a major sixth."

注：level pitch 平坦なピッチ；major 長音階

　Ladd も言っているように、上記のパターンは、親の叱責だけでなく、離れた所にいる人を呼ぶときにも使われる。例えば、相手の名前を呼んだが、返事がないので再び名前を呼ぶ場合である。イギリスで超有名なコメデイーに *Fawlty Towers* という古典的作品があり、Agatha Christy が活躍した保養地 Torquay（南西部）が舞台となっている。この作品では、猛女的女房 Sybil が能天気な夫 Basil を度々甲高い声で呼んでいる。1回目の後、2回目はイライラしたときのイントネーションである。

　"Basil!" The shrill summons from the beast of Torquay...

以下は、文献からである。

　"An impatient caller is apt to vary it (= the calling tune) in the expected direction up, if it is necessary to repeat it:

```
    li        cia !
Fe   cia !  Feli
```

　　　Bolinger, "Intonation in American English" in *Intonation Systems*,
　　　　　　　　　　　　　　　　　　　　ed. by Hirst & Cristo (1998:46)

第 3 章

　この章は、具体的な対話文の朗読練習するところである。英語を学ぶ者が、英語の文を正しく朗読する能力を身に付けようとする際には、ネーティブスピーカーの発音をモデルにして真似るのが妥当な方法である。その際、母音と子音といった個々の音を練習するのも大切ではあるが、それ以上に、プロソディ (prosody) の面を優先するほうがよい。プロソディというのは、話し言葉のアクセント、リズム、イントネーション、ポーズ（休止）の総称である。つまり、個々の音のような細かいことよりも、文という大きなまとまりを「英語らしく」発音する方が得策である。鈴木博は月刊『言語』の中で、「個々の音」対「プロソディ」について、英語のネーティブスピーカーを対象に行った実験の結果を報告している。

　　普通の教育を受けた英語話者の耳には、個々の音が正確で、プロソディが日本語的であるよりも、個々の音は日本語的でも、プロソディが英語的である方が英語らしく聞こえるらしいことが分かったのである。これは、その方がコミュニケーションが容易であることにもつながる。

　　　　　　　　　　　　　　　　　　　　　　　　　　　（1992 年 8 月号）

ネーティブスピーカーの発音をモデルにして真似ると言っても、音声学の基本的な規則を知らずして、mimic（物まね）してもその場限りの練習になってしまうだろう。英語を書いたり読んだりするのに「文法」の知識が欠かせないように、英語を話すためには「音法」が必要である。「音法」と言っても難解な理論ではなく、いわば「教室の音声学」のことである。難しいことはない。John Wells 氏に本書のために書いてもらった序文にある通りのことである。私は、この 20 年間で彼の講義を 10 数回聞いてきたが、イントネーションに限って言うとその趣旨は、いつも同じである。写真は、早稲田大学での講義（2017 年 11 月夕刻）の 1 コマである。

英語のイントネーションを練習するための教材は、ストーリーではなく対話の形式のものにするべきである。しかも、数多くに取り組む。そのほうが、より多様なイントネーションのパターンが学べる。

　文であろうと、独立した句であろうと、その中でどの語が核強勢を受けるかを見極める。音法としては、「右端ルール」に従う、つまり、文や句の末尾から始める。そこは、核強勢を受ける語の定番の位置である。しかし、右端の語が文脈上で既知情報であり、核強勢を受ける資格がないならば、右端から（文頭に向かって）左のほうへ目を移し、適切な candidate を見極める。

　A: What happened? You look frightened.
　B: *I have just seen a GHOST*.
　A: There's no such thing as a ghost.
　B: Well, *I have SEEN a ghost*.
　A: No, you haven't seen a ghost.
　B: Oh yes. *I HAVE seen a ghost*.
　A: Nobody has seen a ghost.
　B: But *I* have seen a ghost.

　右端ルールを通して文中で核強勢を受ける語を見極める練習に慣れ、応用力がついてくると、次のステップは、ネーティブスピーカーのモデル朗読を聴く前に、イントネーションの予想をして、自分の予想とモデル朗読とのズレを試してみるのも進歩につながる。その際、留意するべきは、特定の場面がある教材では、ある１つの文を、複数のネーティブスピーカーが朗読すれば、彼らの間に相違があるということである。場面から独立した文 ─ 例えば、太陽は東から登る、喫煙は健康に害がある等 ─ は、複数の朗読には差がないが、**intonation in context** は、場面の捉え方により、イントネーションに違いが出てくることがある。従って、自分の予想したイントネーションが、モデルと違っていても、予想が間違っていたとは言えないことがある。単なる解釈の違いのこともある。

　この章の Part 1 には、過去数十年のわたる「発音ワークショップ」で利用した教材の中から特に効果的であったものを８点選び、私の友人で大学教授とキリスト教会の司祭の朗読を加えた。

　なお、CD には、３種類の朗読が収録されているが、最初の２つは、ほぼ自然なスピードの朗読である。最後のものは、slower speed の朗読であり、その

ために朗読者（司祭）には苦労をかけてしまった。それ故に多少の不自然さがあるのは否めない。しかし、スピードの違いにより、イントネーションがどのように異なるかを検討するには参考になる音声資料であろう。Part 2 には、朗読の練習をするに際しての留意点の解説がある。なお、その解説の大半は、課題 1 〜 60 の中で扱ったものである。

教室の音声学

Part 1: 朗読課題 🔊

朗読課題 1: Food

  A: Don't you think food in this country is expensive?

  B: Not really.

  A: Well, I think it's expensive.

  B: That's because you eat in restaurants.

  A: Where do *you* eat?

  B: At home.

  A: I didn't know you could cook.

  B: Well, actually I can't cook. I just microwave frozen food.

  A: That's awful.

  B: No, it isn't. I enjoy different kinds of frozen Japanese food.

  A: Frozen food every day? I don't know what to say.

  B: It's inexpensive and delicious. I think it's much better than eating out every day.

朗読課題 2: Zoo

  A: Have you taken your family to the zoo yet, John?

  B: No, but my kids have been asking me to. I've heard this city has a pretty big one.

  A: Yes, it doesn't have a lot of animals, but it does have quite a variety of animals. I think your kids would enjoy seeing the pandas.

  B: I'm sure they would. I'd like to see them, too.

  A: Also, the tigers are worth looking at.

  B: Is it okay to feed them?

  A: No, they're not used to being fed.

  B: What bus do you take to get there?

  A: Number twenty-eight. But don't you have a car?

  B: We used to have one, but we had to sell it.

Part 1: 朗読課題

朗読課題 3: Class reunion

[*Jack and Suzy have run into each other at their 10th-year college reunion.*]

Jack: Suzy? Suzy Jones? Jack Harper. Do you remember me?

Suzy: Jack! How could I forget you? You look just the same — well, maybe a little less hair.

Jack: Oh yeah. And a few more pounds, too! But you're exactly the same. How are you? What've you been doing?

Suzy: Well, I've been in Boston now for four years. I'm managing to support myself, teaching ESL classes. Nothing big yet. But I'm having a great time. What about you? What're *you* doing?

Jack: Well, Chris and I got married right after college. We're living in Seattle. Chris's traveling now, so she couldn't be here today. She's working in a tourist company and she travels a lot.

Suzy: Sounds exciting. What about you?

Jack: Well, I'm between jobs right now. The computer company I was working at went bankrupt recently.

Suzy: I'm sorry to hear that.

Jack: Hey, is that Cathy Simpson? Look how she is surrounded by several guys.

Suzy: She's still just as popular with them as in our college days. Come to think of it, weren't you one of her admirers in those days, too?

朗読課題 4: Red Roses

Lisa: [*Putting down the phone*] That was Samantha on the phone. Honestly, I don't know how she does it.

John: Ah ... Samantha. What's she done now?

Lisa: Nothing, really. That's what's amazing. But somebody has sent her a dozen roses.

John: A dozen what?

Lisa: A dozen roses.

John: Roses ... mmm, I say! And this time of year.

Lisa: Yes. And a dozen roses. He must be keen on her.

John: Is it her birthday or something?

Lisa: No, and what's more, they were red roses.

John: Now ... a dozen red roses. You know what that means?

Lisa: I know what you're going to say.

John: It means he's not just keen. He's in love with her.

Lisa: I know. I know. Poor guy.

John: Poor guy? What do you mean? He doesn't sound poor to me, if he can afford a dozen ...

Lisa: No, I mean I feel sorry for him. He's in love with her — yes. But she's not in love with *him*.

John: How do you know? Did she say so?

Lisa: She doesn't even know who it is, and she says she doesn't really mind. She always manages to deal with such secret admirers.

朗読課題 5: Excuses, Excuses!

[*Peter is a habitual late-comer, and he is late again today. Frank is waiting for him in the waiting room of the station and getting impatient. At last Peter appears. He is full of poor excuses.*]

Frank: Oh, there you are, Peter! At last!

Peter: Sorry to be late, Frank.

Frank: You know, it's pretty cold, waiting here.

Peter: Why didn't you wait in the waiting room? You would have been much warmer there.

Frank: No, I wouldn't. The heating's broken down. Well, now, explain yourself. What's been keeping you this time?

Peter: Oh, it's one of those days. Everything seems to have gone wrong. Take this morning, for instance. Alarm clock fails to go off, miss my train, late for the office, boss early for work for once ...

Frank: Yes, but that was this morning. Why so late now? You're an hour late.

Peter: Well, about fifty minutes.

Frank: No, I make it fifty-*eight* minutes, precisely!

Peter: Well, maybe it was a bit more than fifty. To make a long story short,

Part 1: 朗読課題

before I left the office, the boss wanted to see me about my unpunctuality. His acid comments went on and on.
Frank: And you missed the train again? For the second time today?
Peter: Yes. So you see, it's been a very unlucky day for me.
Frank: I don't know what to say.

朗読課題 6: April Fool！

One April first a bus was running along a country road. It suddenly slowed down and stopped. The driver tried all the switches and buttons, but nothing happened. Then he turned to the passengers. He had a worried look on his face. He said, "This poor bus is getting old. It isn't going well these days. There's only one thing we can try, if we want to go home today."

Then he continued, "I'll count three. When I say 'three', I want you all to lean forward as hard as you can. Then the bus should start again. But if it doesn't, I'm afraid there's nothing else I can do. Now please lean back as far as you can, and be ready."

All the passengers obeyed the driver, and waited.

"One! Two! Three!" counted the driver. The passengers all swung forward suddenly, and the bus started. The passengers looked at each other and smiled.

"April fool!" cried the driver, and laughed. Everyone was taken by surprise. And the next moment they burst into laughter.

朗読課題 7: New York Cab Driver

Driver: Hi. Where to?
Passenger: Times Square, please.
Driver: (on the way) Where're you visiting from?
Passenger: Chicago.
Driver: Yeah, that's what I thought, from the accent.
Passenger: Really? I have an accent. Funny. I never thought about it. Where are *you* from?
Driver: Atlanta.
Passenger: Really? You're from the South? You don't sound Southern.

Driver:	No, of course not. I'm studying to be an actor, and you can't have any accent if you want to be an actor.
Customer:	So you got rid of your Southern accent.
Driver:	That's right. I wiped it out completely.
Customer:	That's interesting. Now you sound like you're from New York.
Driver:	(in shock) I do?

朗読課題 8: *My Ántonia*

They sat looking off across the country, watching the sun go down. The curly grass about them was on fire now. The bark of the oaks turned red as copper. There was a shimmer of gold on the brown river. Out in the stream the sandbars glittered like glass, and the light trembled in the willow thickets as if little flames were leaping among them. The breeze sank to stillness. In the ravine a ringdove mourned plaintively, and somewhere off in the bushes an owl hooted. They sat listless, leaning against each other. The long fingers of the sun touched their foreheads.　　　　出典 Willa Cather, *My Ántonia*

Part 2: 解　説

朗読課題 1: Food

1. ↘Not, ↗really.（課題 46 参照）
2. ↘I think it's expensive.
   - 一番重要な語は I である。これは you との対比である。
   - 再登場の expensive に二次的な重要度を与えたければ、↘I think it's ex↗pensive.
3. ˈWhere do ↘you eat?
4. I ˈdidn't ˈknow you could ↘cook.
   - eat at home と言えば cook を連想させるので、cook が既知内容と見なされる場合、上昇調になる。I ˈdidn't ↘know you could ↗cook.
5. ↘↗Actually | I ↘can't cook.
6. ↘No, it ↗isn't.
   - polite correction のイントネーション（課題 47 参照）。

   類似例

   A: His birthday is May 3.
   B: ↘No, it ↗isn't.
   X: You don't like pork.
   Y: ↘Yes, I ↗do. I eat bacon.

朗読課題 2: Zoo

1. ˈHave you ˈtaken your ˈfamily to the ↗zoo yet, | ↗John?
   - 核強勢は zoo に来る。
   - yet は「時の副詞」であるので、文強勢を受けない。しかし、核強勢のある zoo を起点として始まる上昇調を受け継ぎ高く発音されるので「目立って」聞こえる。
2. ↘No, | but my ↘kids | have been ↘asking me to.
   - 初出の名詞主語は、核強勢を受ける。この文は 2 つの音調単位に分かれる。kids と asking が核強勢を受ける。
   - to は文末にあるので強形 [tu] または [tu:] となる。なお弱形は [tə] である。

3. I've ↘heard | ˈthis ˈcity ⁽¹⁾ has a ˈpretty ↘big one.
   - この文は 2 つの音調単位に分かれる。それぞれに核強勢がある（heard と big）。
   - 文強勢を受ける語が連続し、英語独特の強弱のリズムに乗らないので、中間の位置にある動詞 has を弱めて、口調をよくする。つまり the rule of three が適用される。
   - one は代名詞なので、文強勢を受けない。

4. ↘Yes, | it ˈdoesn't ⁽¹⁾ have a ↘ˈlot of animals, but it ˈdoes have ˈquite a va↘ˈriety of animals.
   - 先行の ˈdoesn't ˈhave（もっていない）に対して ˈdoes have（実際、もっている）なので、doesn't と対比して、does は文強勢を受ける。have は再登場なので文強勢を受けない。
   - animals は既に文脈にあり文強勢を受けないので、核強勢は lot と variety に来る。

5. I think | your ˈkids would enˈjoy ⁽¹⁾ seeing the ↘pandas.
   - 2 つの音調単位に分かれ、それぞれに核強勢がある。
   - enjoy seeing the pandas でも the rule of three が適用され、seeing の強勢が弱められる。

6. I'm ˈsure they ↘would. または I'm ↘sure they would. 前者のほうが、more emphatic. 類似例として、A: Will she come? に対して、
   B₁: I exˈpect she ↘will. または B₂: I ex↘pect she will.

7. ↘I'd like to ˈsee them, | ↘too.
   「子ども」だけでなく「私も」の意味である。言い換えると↘Me, | ↘too.

8. ↘Also, | the ↘tigers are worth looking at.
   - 初出の名詞主語は、いつも核強勢を受ける。
   - worth looking at は、一見すると新情報だが、情報的価値は薄いので、「尾部」になる。そもそも「見る価値のある」動物の話をしている。tigers こそが最重要である。
   - 「尾部」は、下降調の tigers の終結部を引き継ぎ低く発音される。
   - at は、文末にあるので強形 [æt] となる。なお弱形は [ət] である。

9. ↘No, | they're ˈnot ↘used to being fed.
   - fed は、feed と同じ概念と見做し、文強勢を与えないか、または、互

いに違う概念と見做し、文強勢を与えるか。前者の場合には、they're 'not ↘used to being fed となり、後者の場合、they're 'not 'used to being ↘fed。

10. 'What ↘bus do you take | to ↘get there?
    ・2つの音調単位に分かれ、それぞれに核強勢がある。
    ・初出の名詞 bus は、優先的に核強勢を受ける。
11. We ↘used to have one, | but we 'had to ↘sell it.
      have one は have a car と同じ概念であるので、文強勢を受けない。

朗読課題3: Class Reunion
1. 'run into each other　　相互代名詞は文強勢を受けない
2. You 'look (1)just the ↘same.　　強勢音節が3連続なので、中間のものが弱化することが多い。the rule of three が適用される。
3. a 'little (1)less ↘hair
4. a 'few (1)more ↘pounds, | ↘'too.
   ・"in addition" を意味する文末の too は、単独で音調単位を形成するので、核強勢を受ける。
5. Well, I've been in ↘↗Boston now | for 'four ↘years.
   ・2つの音調単位に分かれる。
   ・「ボストンにいること」と「4年間」がそれぞれ major information となる。
6. ... sup↘↗porting myself, ...
   目的語の再帰代名詞は、文強勢を受けない。
7. 'Nothing ↘big yet.
   ・yet は、「時の副詞」として、文末では、通例、文強勢を受けない。
8. I'm 'having a 'great ↘time. OR: I'm 'having a ↘great time.
   ・have a good time とは違い、have a great time では great のほうが強い強勢を受けることがよくある。それは very good の意味があるからであろう。
9. 'What're ↘you doing?　　他者と you との対比。
10. We're 'living in Se↘attle.
    ・We live in Seattle. との違い。進行形は、「とりあえず現在は」の意味。

11. ˈChris's ↘↗ traveling now.　now は「時の副詞」
12. so she ˈcouldn't ↘ be here today.
    しかし、話者に「来る」と対比させる意図がある場合には couldn't に焦点を置く。so she ↘ couldn't be here today.
13. ˈWell, I'm be ↘ tween jobs right now.（失業中）
    仕事のことは、既に話題になっているので、普通、jobs は文強勢を受けない。
14. The comˈputer ˈcompany I was ↘↗ working at | ˈwent ↘ bankrupt recently.
    なお、recently も sentence-final adverbial. である。
15. ˈCome to ↘ think of it,（そう言えば）

朗読課題 4: Red Roses

1　ˈThat was Sa ↘ mantha on the phone.
　・会話の状況を読み取ると、John は Lisa が電話中であることは認識している。on the phone は「場所の副詞句」であるので文強勢を受けず、低い pitch になる。
2　honestly 驚き、苛立ちを表す間投詞
　・Honestly! Do you ever listen?
　Honestly! What a mess you've made!
3　I ˈdon't ⁽¹⁾know ˈhow she ↘ does it.
　・the rule of three が適用
　・誰かの見事な腕前や作品に感心したときに、How does he do it? とか How did she do it? と言う慣用的表現。忙しいにもかかわらず、家事・育児をうまくこなしている人に向かって、"How do you do it?" と言って感心する。
4　ˈWhat's she ˈdone ↘ now? 慣用表現「（あの人に度々驚かされるが）今度は、一体、何をしたのか」
5　↘ Nothing, | ↗ really.
6　ˈThat's what's a ↘ mazing.
　・what は（関係）代名詞であるので、強勢を受けない。
7　a ˈdozen ↘ roses
　・名詞句では名詞のほうが強い強勢を受ける。

Part 2: 解　説

8. A ˈdozen ↗ what? (in surprise)
   - echo question（オウム返し質問）と呼ばれる。
9. I say! (old-fashioned)
   - 慣用表現。相手の発言に対して反応 (reaction) を示す前の「まくら言葉」
10. He ⁽¹⁾must be ↘ keen on her.
    - keen (usually, British usage)「好意を寄せて」の意味。
    - 推量を意味する助動詞は、しばしば強勢を受ける (but not always)
        He ˈmay ↘ come.（～かもしれない）/ He ˈshould be at ↘ ˈhome now.
        （～のはずだ）　推量の may, should, must の強勢は optional である。
11. You ˈknow ˈwhat ↘ that means?
    - 主語の that は、it に対する強意用法として、しばしば強勢を受ける。
        A: I broke my leg.　B: ˈHow did ↘ that happen?
12. Is it her ↗ birthday or something?
13. ˈWhat's ↘↗ more, | they were ↘ red roses.
    - ここでは、red が新情報である。
13. He's ˈnot ⁽¹⁾just ↘ keen.
    - the rule of three が適用。
    - 「単に好意を寄せているだけでなく（行動でも意思表示する）」
14. He ˈdoesn't ⁽¹⁾ sound ˈpoor to ↘↗ me.（または to ↘ me）
    - the rule of three が適用。
    - 他者との対比。「(少なくとも) 私には」
15. But ˈshe is ˈnot in love with ↘ him.
    - 対比の類似例：I ↘ see you and ⁽¹⁾you see ↘ me.
        ˈJim ˈhelped ↘↗ Kate and ⁽¹⁾she helped ↘ him.
16. She ↘ doesn't ⁽¹⁾even ˈknow ˈwho it ↘ is.

朗読課題 5: Excuses, Excuses

1. Oh, ˈthere you ↘ are.
   　ˈHere you ↘ are. (neutral, rather businesslike)
   　ˈHere you ↗ are. (more friendly, more polite)
2. It's ˈpretty ↘ cold, | ˈwaiting ↗ here.
    - このような文構造は、インフォーマルな会話ではよく見られる。下降

＋低上昇調が一般的である。

    a. It can be ↘dangerous, | ↗ski ing.

    b. It's ˈnot ↘comfortable, | ˈgoing in a ˈsmall ↗boat.

    c. It's ˈnot ↘nice, | ˈgetting ↗old.

3. ˈwaiting ˈroom は複合語。

4. You would have been ˈmuch ↘warmer there.

   又は、You would have been ˈmuch ↘warmer | ↗there.

   ・2つの音調単位

   ・「場所の副詞」は、話者が二次的な重要度を与えるときは、独立した音調単位となり、（低）上昇調で言われる。

   類似例：It's a ˈbit ↘cold in here.

          It's a ˈbit ↘cold | in ↗here.

5. The ↘heating's broken down.

   ・event sentence. 名詞が優先的に核強勢を受ける。

   Sorry to be late. My ↘car broke down.

   Quick! The ↘kettle's boiling over!

6. ˈWell now, ex↘plain yourself.

   ・再帰代名詞は動詞の目的語になる場合は、文強勢を受けない。

     She ↘dressed herself.

     She ↘cut herself.

7. it's ˈone of ˈthose ↘days（慣用表現ついてない（不運な）日。）

8. ˈTake ˈthis ↘morning, for instance.

   ・for instance は文末副詞句、文強勢を受けない。

   Let's ˈeat ↘out, for a change. 久しぶりに

9. for once 珍しく

10. I ˈmake it ˈfifty-↘eight minutes, | pre↘cisely.

11. ˌacid ˈcomments (= severe comments)

朗読課題6: April fool

1. a ↘bus | was ˈrunning along…

   ・初出の名詞主語は、独自の音調単位になる。

   類例：A: What happened?　　B: Your ↘sister | ˈhad a ↘car accident.

Part 2: 解　説

2. ˌcountry ˈroad 名詞句　　country club 複合語
3. He ˈhad a ˈworried ↘ look on his face.
   - on his face 場所の副詞句

   類似例：There is a ↘ man at the door.
4. It ˈisn't ↘ going well these days　OR: ... ˈgoing ↘ well　（課題6参照）
5. I ˈwant you ↗ all | to ˈlean ↗ forward | as ˈhard as you ↘ can.
6. ↘↗ Then | the ˈbus ⁽¹⁾ should ↘ start again.
   - should は推量の意味。「～のはずだ、きっと～だろう」
   - again は、「元のように」「元どおりに」意味で、文強勢を受けない。
7. "One! Two! Three!" counted the driver.
   - counted the driver は「尾部」であるので低く発音される。独自の音調単位にはならない。
8. The ˈpassengers ↘ looked at each other.
   - 相互代名詞は、目的語の場合、文強勢を受けない。
9. "April fool!" cried the driver.
   - cried the driver. は、尾部である。独自の音調単位にはならない。
   - ˈApril ↗↘ ↗ fool (rise-fall-rise)

朗読課題 7: New York Cab Driver

1. ˈWhere ↘ to?
   - 類例　A: I'm saving money.
   　　　　B: ˈWhat ↘ for? For a rainy day?
2. I ˈnever ↘ thought about it.
   - cf. A: Did you ever think about it?
   　　　B: ↘ No, I ↘ never thought about it.
3. ˈWhere are ↘ you from?
4. You ˈdon't ↘ sound Southern.
   - または、再登場の southern に二次的重要度を与えると

   You ˈdon't ↘ sound | ↗ Southern.

   類例：A: Do you like *sushi*?　　B: ↘ Yes, I ↘ like | ↗ *sushi*.
5. I ↗ do? または、I ↗↘↗ do? (more emphatic)

朗読課題 8: *My Ántonia*

　19 世紀後半、ヨーロッパのボヘミアからアメリカの開拓地ネブラスカに移住してきた家族の物語。特にアントニアという女性の生涯を描いている。女流作家 Willa Cather の代表作。この朗読資料は、夕暮れ時のネブラスカの景色が、色彩画のように美しく描写されている。

まとめ

　自然な英語発音を身に付けるには、そのリズムとイントネーションの練習が必要であると言われている。英語のリズムにおけるkey factorは「等時性」(equal stress timing)であり、イントネーションにおけるkey factorは「核強勢」である。等時性とは、強勢のある部分が一定の間隔で現れる現象を意味している。

　ˈCome.
　ˈCome to ˈtea.
　ˈCome to ˈtea with ˈJohn.
しかし、リズム練習は、ほどほどにしないといけない。

　実は、このようなリズムの練習は、自信喪失や英語嫌いを産む要因の1つである。ある日、英語の教師が書いた記事を見かけた。

　　「私が中学生の時の英語の先生は北米に留学されていた方で、自然な教室英語を駆使していたように記憶しているが、中1の1学期中間考査の後くらいで、やっと文らしいものが出てくると、指し棒で机を叩いて、このようなリズムをとりながら音読練習をさせていた。これが嫌だった。当時の私には、この等時性を強要されるのが不快だったのだ。それ以来、中3の12月まで英語の授業が嫌で嫌でしょうがなかった。自分が教師になってからもこの等時性を強要したことはない。中学校の先生などで、メトロノームやリズムボックスを使う人がいるが、本当に生徒に喜ばれているか考えてみて欲しい。」

　英語のリズム練習でよく使われる手法は、チャンツ（chants）である。小学校での英語活動で使われていた『英語ノート』（文科省配布）には、チャンツが多くあった。しかし、意味も分からず、お遊戯的で幼稚な活動には、高学年の子どもは乗ってこない。極めて悪評である。狙いは、学童期の段階から英語のリズムを体感させようとすることだろうが、幼い子供が言語を習得する（acquire）プロセスと、外国語として学習する（learn）プロセスとを混同している。しかも、日常会話では、必ずしも規則的なリズムになるとは限らない。equal timingだけの英語を聞くと、何とも不自然である。

　　"And it seems sometimes that some writers on English pronunciation assume that really we're talking like that all the time, but sometimes you can't quite make out the rhythm... In ordinary conversational speech, you

can't hear that. It is difficult to pick up regular rhythmical patterns."
Peter Roach, 講演（東京、1997）

　規則的なリズムが現われるのは、詩や nursery rhyme などの韻文の中である。詩をつくる場合、<u>意図的に規則正しい</u>リズムが生まれるように語を配置するが、日常会話の場合には、とっさの発言であるので、しばしばリズムは不規則になる。音声学の教科書には以下のような例を見かけることがある。

a. ˈDogs ˈeat ˈbones.
b. ˈDogs will ˈeat ˈbones.
c. The ˈdogs will ˈeat the ˈbones.
d. The ˈdogs will have ˈeaten the ˈbones.

過去には、a～d は同じ強勢音節数なので、各文の間には時間差がほとんど存在しないという指導が行われてきたが、実際には、a から d に移行するにつれて発話時間が長くなることが実証されている。それにもかかわらず、equal stress timing を強要するのは百害あって一利なしである。

　そう言えば、かつて、GDM セミナーで、参加者の 1 人（女性、教員）が、東京の M 大学での夏期発音講座に出席したが、リズムに関するセッションがいかに精神的苦痛であり、自信喪失になったかを切々と語られた。受講料を数万も払ったので、最後まで我慢して出席したが、何も身に付かなかったと。私は、他の人たちからも類似の体験談を度々聞いている。perfect model を前にして、焦りとストレスが高まる。機械的に英語を発する練習は卑屈であり、非生産的である。英語のリズム練習は、どちらかと言えば単純で、お遊戯的で、非知的活動である。それ故に、本を執筆するのは比較的易しい。それ故に、「英語はリズムだ！」とかそれに類したタイトルの本を書店でよく見かける。

　一方、イントネーションは、話し手と聞き手との interplay であり、絶えず context（*sen-sit*）に大きく依存しているので、その練習は大人の活動、知的活動である。イントネーションの練習でも、音法を知った上で自分の思考回路を経なければ上達は望めない。単なる mimicry では効果がない。しかも、あるイントネーションのパターンを実際の文脈の中で生かせる（応用する）ようになるまでに、数か月、時には、1、2 年もの「熟成」の期間が必要であろう。最初のうちは、ある音調が下降調であるのか、それとも上昇調であるのか、或いは、下降・上昇調であるのかを聞き分けることも決してたやすいことではな

いかもしれない。その意味で、同じ内容のレクチャーを、2，3回ぐらい聞くと、その都度、少し霧が晴れるように新しい「発見」があり、理解の深化につながるだろう。実際、何か新しいことを学んでも、脳裏に刷り込まれるには、反芻の期間が必要である。本書にある「教室の音声学」よりも先に進みたい人には、John Wells, *English Intonation*（2006）をお薦めしたい。学問的・教育的意義が高い福音書である。主として日本英語音声学会会員による翻訳書（研究社）から出ている。日本人学習者に理解しやすい文章で書かれている。また、CDもついている。

あとがき

本書の出版を考え始めたのは、2017年の11月にJohn Wells氏が早稲田大学で講演をされ、夕方、懇親会で同じテーブルで談笑したことがきっかけであった。その席で、Wells氏から、「Tami, あなたは、これまで私の講義を何度も聞いてきたのだから、receiveばかり  しないで何かgiveしたらどうかね」という言葉があったからである。この言葉の背景には、彼の著書 *English Intonation* のprefaceでの次の文章がある。

I have benefitted from many discussions over the years with my colleagues Michael Ashby, Patricia Ashby, Jill House and John Maidment. Email discussions on the Supras list were stimulating, particularly the input from Tamikazu Date...

宴席であったので、冗談で言われたのかもしれないが、その言葉が、それ以降ずっと脳裏の片隅に残っていた。折も折、日本英語音声学会が23年の歴史を閉じ、日本実践英語音声学会が発足することになり、自らも何か区切りとなる企画として、今回の出版に踏み切ることにした。

次の皆様方にはお世話になった。ゲラの校正には、常磐会学園大学教授Bill Rockenbach氏と芦屋聖マルコ教会の佐藤耕一氏に協力していただいた。また、録音は、同教会の司祭Warren Wilson氏とRockenbach氏が引き受けてくださった。感謝の念に堪えない。

最後になるが、本書を出版する機会を与えてくださった大阪教育図書社長の横山哲彌氏と制作部の土谷美知子氏に深く御礼申し上げる。

経　歴

著者　伊達　民和

　　大阪市立大学文学部卒業、関西外国語大学大学院修士課程修了（英語学修士）、文部省派遣教員としてキャンベラ大学（オーストラリア）教育学部留学（2 semesters）。職歴として、大阪府立高校英語科教諭（3校）、大阪府教育委員会事務局高等学校課指導主事（7年）、常磐会短期大学教授を経てプール学院大学教授、定年退職。

　　主な著書として、『英語のリズム・イントネーションのトレーニング法──理論から実戦へ』（青山社、1998）、『映画・ドラマから学ぶ英語音法読本』（青山社、2001）、主な共著として、『英語の Listening Box 1, 2, 3』シリーズ（啓林館、2005）、*English in Singapore ── Phonetic Research on a Corpus*（McGraw-Hill, 2005）、『現代音声学・音韻論の視点』（金星堂、2012）、翻訳・監訳書として、元・ローマカトリック教会ドミニコ会総長 Timothy Radcliffe 著『なぜ教会に行くのか──パンとぶどう酒のドラマ』（聖公会出版、2013）、同著者『なぜクリスチャンになるのか』（教文館、2016）、第104代カンタベリー大主教 Rowan Williams 著『信頼のしるし』（教文館、2017）。

校閲・朗読　Bill Rokenbach

　　Bill Rockenbach was born and raised in the U.S. state of North Dakota. He received a BS degree in mathematics and botany at Iowa State University in Ames, IA, and an MS in mathematics from Cornell University in Ithaca, NY. After coming to Japan in 1980, he has worked in the field of English education and taught at the Osaka YMCA and Tokiwakai Junior College, and he is now a professor at Tokiwakai Gakuen University. He has been a member of the development teams for the government-approved *Voice*, *Vivid*, *Viva* and *Perspective* series of English textbooks published by Daiichi Gakushuusha. Bill's interests and hobbies include education in general, linguistics, the life sciences, cycling, jogging and languages, including Japanese and Russian. He considers it a privilege and great honor to have been able to work with Professor Date as a colleague and on numerous other occasions at the YMCA, Tokiwakai and elsewhere over the many years of their professional and personal acquaintance.

教室の音声学読本
―― 英語のイントネーションの理解に向けて ――

2019年5月30日　初版第1刷発行

著　者　伊達　民和
発行者　横山　哲彌
印刷所　西濃印刷株式会社

発行所　大阪教育図書株式会社
　　　　〒530-0055　大阪市北区野崎町1-25
　　　　TEL 06-6361-5936　　FAX 06-6361-5819
　　　　振替 00940-1-115500

ISBN978-4-271-41026-3 C3082　　　落丁・乱丁本はお取り替え致します。

本書のコピー、スキャン、デジタル化等の無断複製は著作権法上での例外を除き禁じられています。本書を代行業者等の第三者に依頼してスキャンやデジタル化することは、たとえ個人や家庭内での利用であっても著作権法上認められておりません。